D0978634

Performance Anxiety

Creating A Fortune Investing in
Non-Performing Real Estate Loans

Gordon Moss
Copyright © 2014 Gordon Moss

Dedication

To my father, Gordon Sr.

Contents

About the Author:

Gordon Moss began his real estate career in 1985 as a commercial real estate broker in Orange County, California.

He has been an avid student of the masters of all facets of the real estate and investing business for over 25 years.

Gordon now owns and manages a portfolio of properties and notes full-time, and is very passionate and active in what he believes is the best real estate and note investment opportunity we will see in our lifetimes.

These 25 years of experience and focus give a unique perspective, and Gordon takes great pride in the fact that he has a unique ability to make money in any real estate market.

Over the last several years he has studied, developed, refined, and mastered several creative techniques that have allowed him to prosper and grow while avoiding the land mines in a very challenging and risky declining marketplace.

Additionally, he has dusted off a few time tested methods of building a fortune that work now better than they ever did – but are overlooked or not understood by the real estate and note investing community.

He enjoys writing, speaking, and mentoring serious investors as a way for him to give back, as his mentors did for him.

He is a published author in several key industry

publications and frequent speaker and panelist at real estate, note, and investment clubs and meetings.

Visit RealEstateAndNoteInvesting.com for a special message from Gordon

Acknowledgement

There have been so many that have inspired and motivated me - I want to thank all of them. They gave me the courage and confidence to take the game of life and my real estate and note investment endeavors to the next level.

Chapter One:

The Best and Safest "High-Return" Investment I Know Of

I've traveled all over the country and almost everyone I've met has shared a similar desire...No matter who you are, or how much money you make, you probably want to make more and ultimately achieve financial independence.

Everyone, from the kid flipping burgers at the local fast food joint to the guy sitting at the top of a fortune 500 company, wants to make enough money to live their dreams. I suppose this is why investing has always been such a popular topic.

Investing fills this need in a unique way. If done well, It gives the ability to "replace one's self".

Instead of working day after day, you can invest a little bit of money and have it earn you even more and maybe even begin to compound the profits.

With enough patience and good investments, you can generate a healthy stream of income to replace your income from your job or profession.

The Quest

In the early years of the last decade we experienced a cyclical housing boom. Property values were incredibly high and housing development was going on all over the country. People were taking out loans, buying up houses, and reducing available inventory.

All of this, however, eventually came crashing down and everyone who had participated in this speculative real estate bubble received a rather rude awakening.

We were suddenly faced with a situation where housing prices were dropping precipitously. Many people had purchased a house which was now rapidly depreciating only a few years later.

The loans they had taken out were much higher than what they could afford. Since the houses were now worth less than the loan balances, there was very little these borrowers could do.

These borrowers stopped paying back their mortgages, which caused banks to stop creating new mortgages. The pool of available real estate buyers began to shrink, and property values dropped even farther. We were in the midst of a crisis and the entire economy was feeling the effect.People lost their jobs, businesses downsized, and paychecks were cut. This made the problem even worse and there was soon a glut of delinquent mortgages. This caused the banks to do the only thing they knew how – foreclose.

Foreclosures began flooding the market. The banks were repossessing the collateral used on these loans and were liquidating the properties at incredibly drastic discounts.

What we were seeing was a huge abundance of these foreclosed properties. The prices for these properties were so much lower than their original fair market value that many investors couldn't resist. They started buying up the foreclosed properties.

As a 25 year real estate investor, I felt the allure myself. Some of these were very nice properties... houses for which at a different time, I would have paid many times more than the bank was asking.

Something held me back, however, and it took me some time to figure out what it was.

More importantly, there was no clear way to make a short term profit from them. People were buying these houses in the hope that property values would go back up.

While we may be seeing some economic recovery, many times, there is no way to know when you will be able to make a quick profit from a foreclosed property.

Worse yet, many of these properties were located in towns which had been hit especially hard by the housing bubble.

These were towns which had lost major businesses - towns which relied on high property values to keep the area desirable. It will take much more than a slight increase in the value of a house to help pull these towns out of the downturn.

I soon realized these foreclosed properties were going to be an exceedingly long term investment, which required continued maintenance and expenses for years to come.

I have been and will always be a long term "buy and hold" real estate investor and did buy some of the best rental houses in my portfolio with amazing low interest, 30 year financing during this time.

But, I wanted to find a way to capitalize on the current situation even more with a short term "lower risk" income producing strategy. While others were seeing this economic downturn as a disaster, *I knew deep down inside that it was an opportunity*.

There was some way to make money in this market, and it was something most other people were not doing. I knew there was a hidden niche just waiting to be broken open.

I began thinking about the main causes of this crisis. The obvious problem was that housing prices were dropping all over the country. Ordinarily, this shouldn't affect mortgages because if someone is approved for a loan then it's safe to assume that they have been prequalified for it and they have the resources to pay it back.

The real problem was that people didn't have the money to pay their monthly mortgages because they had been given a loan they really couldn't afford and were experiencing job losses and related financial challenges during the great recession.

The banks had become a bit *"overzealous"* in underwriting these new loans. These loans had zero or less down payments, variable adjusting interest rates, negative amortization, weak underwriting requirements, and other exciting terms which began to inflate and implode as the economy grew worse.The farther down the economy plummeted, the higher the payments grew on many of these mortgages. Eventually people could no longer pay them. This was a problem which escalated until the banks had so many delinquent loans they had no idea what to do with them.

A lot of my friends had been purchasing foreclosed and REO properties through the "front door" at the bank, but I decided to go up a bit farther down the ladder.

When someone purchases a house, they will usually take out a loan from the bank. This loan has a contract which needs to be signed. The contract is also called a note secured by a deed of trust or mortgage.

The key to my epiphany came to me when I realized that *banks don't want to foreclose on their notes.*

These banks are in the business of making money by offering loans. They don't want to own physical real estate—especially when foreclosing on some properties can take years, and can be very politically challenging.

If they had the choice, the banks would much rather receive the payments on their loans. At the very least, they want to make back a bit of the money they lost when their loan stopped performing.

The only reason these banks were foreclosing was to recover some of the money they lost on these bad loans. As the delinquent loans began to pile up, however, there was just no way they could foreclose on every home and they were even prohibited by the government in many cases.

What I discovered is that to solve the problem quickly, these banks will often sell off their delinquent notes. They were effectively selling the loan contracts and transferring/assigning the ownership to anyone that purchased them.

The Niche

I began to do a lot of research. I called people, traveled to mortgage and loan events all over the country, talked to banks, and I read through mountains of information.I soon learned it was entirely possible to purchase these notes from the bank. As long as you could prove you were a serious, credible and experienced loan investor, the banks would sell you a number of their non-performing loans.

This was an intriguing prospect. It would allow me to essentially invest in something purchased at a discount (a note) with collateral which was valued as highly as a single family house.I would be able to make that money back if I could get these borrowers to settle or start paying off their loan.

Also, *I wouldn't have to worry about any property maintenance or tenant hassles because I wasn't purchasing properties—just the note tied to that property.*

The secret to making a profit from these investments would be my ability to work with these borrowers building "win/win" solutions and convince them to begin paying off their loans.

I'm an optimistic person and I was fairly confident that I'd be able to do exactly that. I've worked with all sorts of people and I'm a problem solver. I like to find solutions and I'm good at it.

The investment capital needed to start buying these discounted non performing senior notes was substantial – even though these notes were non performing (not paying) the banks had priced them at a premium. It was more than I thought I should pay.

More importantly, it was higher than I thought most defaulted borrowers could pay back on their notes.

Another problem I faced was that these notes were only sold in large collections (or pools). These pools of notes, could cost millions of dollars and were usually sold to the highest qualified bidder in an auction environment.

Since all of the notes I had been looking at were first lien mortgages, they would have been expensive even if I managed to buy them individually.

I soon realized something which set me on a new course. Nearly everyone who has ever purchased a house had to take out a first mortgage.

Quite a few more people have also taken out a **second**

mortgage (a junior lien) for additional capital for other improvements or expenses secured by their home.

These seconds were often much smaller than the first. Since they are in a position that is junior to the first mortgage—meaning the first is at the head of the line—most people did not see them as a secure and safe investment and thus were not bidding on and investing in them.

The reason for this is that most lenders (senior lien holders) were threatening foreclosure at the time.

Since the second mortgage loan balances are relatively low, and is technically subservient to the first, most of the larger investors were wary of the risk of being "wiped out" (loss of lien position through foreclosure process) by a foreclosing senior lien and were ignoring these junior loans.

My plan was different - I didn't want to foreclose and take over the property. I owned enough properties and was looking for a different angle.

Pricing is key – The main difference that attracted me to these second liens was that they were priced so much lower (almost like an option) than the delinquent first liens.

While I could possibly buy a quality "sand state" (CA, AZ, NV, etc.) non performing first lien for about 70 or 80 cents on the dollar, there were many "quality" non performing junior liens which I could buy for less than 10, 20, or 30 cents on the dollar.

The discount for the junior liens was so incredible, I felt there was no way I could fail to make a profit if I could get them worked out or performing once again.

So far, I was convinced, but there still seemed to be one major problem standing in my way. When banks sell off

7

their notes, they do so in huge pools. These pools could consist of hundreds or thousands of different notes which were tied to different borrowers all over the country.

I had neither the resources nor desire to invest at this level. Since I was new to this market, I didn't want to over extend and find myself with a huge collection of potentially worthless paper.

What I found was that most banks will sell these pools to hedge funds. These are groups of investors who have raised investor capital in an effort to invest in what they perceive as large current market opportunities.

For the most part, many of these hedge funds were not fixing the notes. They were simply breaking them up into smaller pools and reselling them. Some of these smaller pools were then purchased and resold to smaller hedge funds or private investors (like me).

What this process did was continually decrease the size and overall purchase price of these note pools. I realized that if I got in at the right level I could then purchase only those notes I felt were a wise investment.

I would be able to pick and choose only those notes which fit my criteria and would hopefully make me a healthy return.

That was the final step I needed. I had found an investment which was both affordable and offered a high potential for profit.

The cost of these notes was so low, in fact, that I could buy a $20,000 loan for about $2,000.

I figured if I could work with the borrower and get them paying again, I would potentially be able to make over $15,000 on that particular note.

Since the price was so affordable and there seemed to be an abundance of these junior notes, I could do it over and over again.

The Process

The workout process is the skill you must master – the skill the banks do not have. The only reason the banks have gotten rid of their notes is because the borrowers aren't paying them off.

Some of these notes have been delinquent for a number of years and the borrower is not going to start paying you money simply because you bought their loan.

The most important element in this strategy is working with the borrower.

Before you even start looking at notes, you need to get out of the mindset that says these are just pieces of paper. Each note represents a different borrower with their own personal story and life problems.

Many of these are honest, hard-working people who simply got caught up in a very complex financial situation. When you purchase a note, you are effectively buying the ability to help these people out of one of the hardest periods in their lives.

These borrowers are behind on their debts. They are probably receiving cancellation notices and may have to hide from bill collectors.   More importantly, your borrowers are facing the very real possibility of being evicted from their home.

This is where you, as a note investor, come in. You are the light at the end of the tunnel. You're the one who will offer them a way out of this problem.

The process is fairly simple. When I first buy a note, I will begin collecting all of the information I can about the borrower. I can find credit reports, litigation history and even personal information from a variety of resources.

The point of this step is to learn about my borrower and find a way to contact them.

The next step is to try contacting them. If I'm able to get hold of the borrower, I will then try to explain the situation.

An informed borrower is much easier to work with, so I will try to present as much pertinent information as I can.

I tell them who I am, how I bought the note, and what I intend to do with it. I'm always very up front and honest. I let them know I intend to get them to start paying back their loan.

I have had a lot of people wonder how anyone could make money from a non-performing junior lien. If this person has not been paying back their loan when the bank owned it, why would they start paying me?

The secret is that I can offer them *a much better solution* than the bank. My goal is not to foreclose but to keep them in their house. I want them to get out of this tough situation and into one which works for them.

The reason investing in non-performing junior liens works is because you are actually helping these borrowers. I've managed to purchase this loan for a fraction of its value.

This puts me in a much more malleable position than the bank. I have a number of different options to offer my borrowers and the discount I've received has made this possible.

Now that I own their loan, I can modify it so that it fits in with their budget. I can turn their eminent foreclosure into a loan which they can afford to pay back.

This can be done in a number of ways and different solutions work for different borrowers.

One option I have is extending the length of the loan.

Turning a 10-year loan into a 30-year loan can cut the monthly payments by a third of the original cost.

Another option would be reducing the interest rate from 8% to 3%, which would also reduce the cost of the monthly payments. There have been some cases where I've managed to reduce a borrower's payments from $800 a month to only $350.

Think of how valuable that would be to someone... very few banks are going to do that for them.

In my experience, most borrowers are more than happy to start paying me after I've modified their loan. You have to realize this is something these people have been praying for.

They are so far in debt there is nothing they can do. The only way out is through some sort of miracle. These people have dealt with greedy debt collectors and inhuman banks for so long they have started to lose hope.

When you offer a borrower a solution like this, you are creating a mutually beneficial situation. As your borrower begins paying back their loan, their credit will improve.

Once they pass a certain point, their mortgage has actually become current again and they're no longer behind. They're free from the worry of foreclosure and can finally begin rebuilding their own credit rating.

You've basically given them a ladder they can use to climb out of that dark pit they've found themselves in.

At this point in the process, you're already making money. A re-performing note usually needs very little work and so this income is almost entirely passive.

More importantly, the deep discount you got when purchasing the note means you will pay off your investment cost in record time and will be soon collecting a profit.

If you wanted, you could simply leave the note alone and continue collecting payments until it's been paid off.

The Path to Profits

This is the most basic process for investing in notes. You will buy a note, contact the borrower, develop a solution, and then start collecting payments.

There is, of course, a lot more detail to it and this book will cover every piece of information as thoroughly as possible.

As you progress through this book, you will also learn some valuable tips and tricks which can help improve your chances of success.

The Shock and Awe Package, for example, is something I've developed and found to be very effective at solving a number of common problems.

You will learn all about this package and a variety of other techniques in the coming chapters.

On top of this, you will also discover a number of different effective exit strategies. My goal has always been to make as much money as I can as quickly as possible.

With this in mind, I've come up with a number of great tactics which speed things up and increase the speed with which you make your money.

This book is the culmination of several decades worth of experience investing in real estate and notes. I've worked with people all over the country and have handled investments of all types.

Non-performing junior liens are my preferred investment today and, as you read, you will learn why.

This is a *very* exciting and highly profitable niche market that very few people know about and even fewer really understand.

12

With the information presented in these pages and patient persistence, you'll be empowered with the knowledge to become successful in this niche in your own right over time.

The Important Questions (and Answers)

When I speak to groups and associations of note and real estate investors, I am often asked the same questions over and over again.

I can also think of nine questions that aren't asked as often, but are also very important in understanding why non-performing notes are such a great opportunity, and how the process works from beginning to end.

I'm going to list those questions here and answer them briefly. Each one is covered in depth elsewhere in this book, and I will let you know which chapter you can go to for the full explanation.

The Eight Most Frequently-Asked Questions About Non-Performing Notes:

1. *Why Non Performing Notes, Why Now, and Why Non Performing JUNIOR Liens?*

   (See Chapter 2): Because you can buy them for 10 cents on the dollar or less - non-performing notes cost less to purchase than larger investments like real estate, so the small investor has a chance to earn a return *several times higher* than stocks, bonds, mutual funds, etc.

   There is currently a large supply of these notes with less competition working against you because similar investors are fighting over first mortgages or the properties themselves, which you don't have to.

2. *Isn't This Extremely Risky? And How Long Will This Opportunity Last?*

(See Chapter 2) It is very low-risk if you screen and purchase your notes properly. When you buy something for 10% of its face value, secured by real estate with a decent amount of equity, from someone who displays signs that they are able and willing to work something out with you, it's hard to fail in most cases if you know what you are doing.

(See Chapter 3) This opportunity will last for at least a few more years from the time of this writing, because there is still a glut of non-performing loans left over from the real estate/financial crisis.

After that, there will not be as many of them, but it is still a very viable investment strategy – as there will always be non- performing junior liens.

3. *Where Do I Find These Notes, And How Much Do I Pay?*

(See Chapter 3) It takes more time and commitment than shopping around online, I suggest meeting and building relationships with bankers and people in this financial industry.

Once they know and trust you, they will come to you directly with notes to purchase, and you won't have competition or be forced to purchase enormous packages all at once when you only want a few carefully-chosen notes.

The better you understand this unique marketplace the better pricing and selection you will recognize and capture.

4. *Why Would They Sell These Notes To Me?*

(See Chapter 1) As mentioned earlier, banks are in

the business of making loans and doing minimal servicing and collections. Once a borrower is behind in payments, the lender will make a few attempts to collect, and then they simply want the loan off of their books.

They are also prohibited from making new loans until a certain ratio of good-to-bad loans is cleaned up on the balance sheet. They are ready to take their losses and move on, and smaller lenders would love a trusted, competent buyer like yourself to take a few loans off of their hands as needed.

5. *What Is The Process To "Work Out" These Loans?*

(See Chapters 6 & 7) These chapters will go into detail about how I first "wake-up" the borrower by contacting them by mail, phone, door-knocking, etc., in order to start the conversation and let them know I intend to collect.

Once that is done, I do my best to negotiate a "work-out" with them—in other words, making payment arrangements with them one way or another.

This could mean monthly payments to me, or arranging for them to refinance or sell the house and pay off the loan if possible.

6. *What If The Borrower Files Bankruptcy Or I Have To Foreclose?*

(See Chapter 8) Bankruptcy is not as big of a problem as you might think. Keep in mind that your equity investment is secured by real estate and is not going to get wiped out like unsecured debts such as a credit card debt would.

When a borrower files Chapter 13, they have to fill out a detailed plan on how they are going to pay it back. The court reviews it and appoints a Trustee to make sure things go on schedule.

And as it turns out, not many borrowers in bankruptcy complete their proposed plan. When it falls through, they are out of bankruptcy and you're back where you started again.

(See Chapter 9) I usually start out by mentioning that I'm willing to foreclose, to encourage the borrower to take action.

If you get no response, go ahead and start the foreclosure proceedings by getting a company to file a Notice of Default for you, such as an attorney or trustee company.

The majority of the time, the borrower will contact you in order to avoid losing their house, and then you can cancel or postpone the process.

7. *What Are The Most Common Exit Strategies, And What Are My Options Once I Fix Or "Re-perform" These Notes?*

The most common exit strategy is working out a payment plan. In todays market, borrowers usually can't get a refinance loan and pay you off.

They're usually not interested in selling their house, though sometimes that happens, and you get paid at that time (either in full or partially, if you help them to do a short sale).

But typically, you can modify their loan balance and/or payment amount to something that's affordable for them, and then collect payments until you have gotten your money back and then some.

You can also sell off *part* of your note to an investor for extra cash, and divide the future payments received with the investor.

8. *Can I Do This In My Self-Directed IRA?*

(See Chapter 11) You absolutely can, and this is what I do because I'm in this game for the long run and making the most money over time (and paying the least in taxes). I buy my notes with funds in my self-directed Roth IRA.

The Nine Questions You Should Be Asking About Non-Performing Notes:

1. *Where Have These Notes Been Before I Have Purchased Them?*

(See Chapter 1) The loans are very often hedge funds assets which they control and sometimes have tried to collect on.

You want to make sure to buy the fresh ones direct from the bank that they have not tried to work in the last 6 months or longer... or notes that have been bought, sold, and worked on 3-4 times.

In the end, it really comes down to how good you are at collecting and what price you negotiate with any note acquisition.

2. *Why Is A Complete Understanding Of The "Emotional Equity" Concept So Important In Buying Non-Performing Junior Liens?*

(See Chapter 4) Emotional Equity helps you predict which notes are truly the most likely to be successfully collected and re-performed. Investors who do not understand this concept will not buy many non-performing junior liens.

They play it safe and stick to the limited quantity of full equity notes. By focusing on less-than-pristine notes, you can get some amazing deals and not pass over the best investments.

In this book, you will learn certain signs that a borrower is emotionally attached to their home and will fight to keep it despite their current setbacks.

3. *Am I Able To Develop Relationships With The Key Players In This Niche – And Why Is This SO Important?*

    (See Chapter 5) This business is about relationships - not spreadsheets. The best way to find notes to purchase is by getting to know the people in a position to sell them to you.

    This can take a lot of time...it took me many trips and visits to note and lending association meetings, taking key people to lunch, etc.

    But your hard work will pay off, as there's nothing like getting a phone call from a friend with a handful of excellent notes to have first pick at buying.

4. *What Are The Real Statistics On Borrowers That File And Complete Their Bankruptcy Filings – And Why Is This Important?*

    (See Chapter 8) Believe it or not, only 10% of borrowers who file bankruptcy end up completing the process. When I ask people to guess this at speaking events, very few people guess correctly how low it really is.

    What this means for you is that, should the borrower file bankruptcy when you're trying to collect on a note, that you'll have to wait a little longer before attempting to collect *your way*, but in all likelihood you will either begin receiving payments of some kind from the trustee as part of the bankruptcy, or that you'll just have to wait it out for a while but not lose your asset.

5. *Is There Any Way A Busy Professional Can Participate In This Opportunity?*

Investing in non-performing notes takes a lot of *calendar time*, but not a lot of your daily *personal time*, if that makes sense.

Your time investment, once you have secured relationships with lenders and people in a position to refer you to notes for sale, is limited to screening a handful of notes here and there, making the purchase, contacting the borrower multiple times, and then collecting a check or payment each month (which can be automated).

6. *What is The Current State Of The Market In Terms Of Foreclosing First Mortgages And Appreciating Or Declining Values In The Country And Why Is That Important?*

(See Chapter 3) In today's market, first mortgages are not getting foreclosed on by lenders, and this trend is moving across the country.

The worst exposure for you as a junior lien holder is if there is little equity and the first mortgage forecloses and you get wiped out. Another good sign is that appreciation is happening again in the current housing market, so you get in a safer position (phantom note appreciation) with each passing month that prices rise.

7. *Would You Recommend An Aggressive or Not Approach To Working Out These Loans?*

(See Chapters 6 & 7) Lately, I have had a much less

aggressive approach because I am a long-term player and feel the long term profits are substantially greater.

The notes are usually paid back one way or another (did you know the average person only lives in their home for 7 years?) With the market getting hotter again and having bought at a huge discount, I have plenty of time to wait to get paid back.

Nevertheless, you should let the borrower know you are serious and would consider foreclosure with your Shock and Awe package and initial phone conversations with them.

8. *Is Outsourcing The Collections And Servicing A Possibility?*

(See Chapter 10) You can get a collection company to call and attempt a work-out for you once you've bought a note, but it usually doesn't work.

This is a high-touch personal relationships business, and $10/hour people never seem to get it right.

Sometimes partnering with another investor who is skilled at doing work-out arrangements can pay off, but you have to split the profits with them and I have found the real path to success here is just to get good at working out deals myself.

9. *How Can Investing In A Non Performing Junior Lien Possibly Be Considered The "Least Risky" Investment Strategy Available To The Small Investor Today?*

(See Chapter 2) In a nutshell... you have more control than stocks and mutual funds, less management hassle and expensive things that can go wrong as with real estate investing, and the initial purchase price is very, very LOW which means potential large returns when you collect.

CHAPTER TWO:

Why Non-Performing _JUNIOR_ Liens?

I like to consider myself an average investor. My goals are essentially the same as any other investor, regardless of what they might invest in.I'm always looking for an affordable, low-risk investment which will make me a healthy return. I want to _spend as little as possible up front_ and not have to _worry too much_ about each investment.

Real estate, has been my investment of choice for many decades. I have bought and sold and held many properties over the years and did well doing so.No matter how much I made, however, I couldn't help but think there had to be a better way. I was convinced there was a better investment out there, one which cost less to purchase but offered a greatly increased short term profit margin.

I was eventually introduced to the world of delinquent notes. Like most people, I was skeptical and confused about this topic. I didn't understand why anyone would buy a delinquent loan and I had no idea how someone would make money from one.If there was money to be made, I thought, why would the banks sell the note in the first place?

As I gained more experience and came to understand

the note market, I started to see how great of an investment notes can really be. I decided to get specific and focus on one note market in particular.The majority of my attention has been on non-performing junior liens which are tied to a single family residence, owner occupied homes all across the country.There are a great variety of different notes but this book will explain why non-performing junior liens are in my opinion, the best option.

What is a Non-Performing Junior Lien?

The first problem most people have is they simple don't understand what a non-performing junior lien really is. The answer is quite simple and will help begin to illuminate why they are such a great investment.The notes this book will focus on are notes secured by a mortgage or deed of trust in second position on a single-family residential property.

Many people will purchase a house at some point in their life. Most people, however, don't actually have the cash on hand to purchase the house in full.They will need to take out a loan with which they can purchase the house and then pay off the loan in small incremental monthly payments. This payment plan can often last for many decades and will be a continuing expense to the homeowner.

The primary (usually larger loan) used for the main acquisition is done and recorded "first" on the property and a borrower may apply for and get a "second" loan (usually a smaller amount and recorded after the first) to assist with a part of the original acquisition cost or later for home improvements or other expenses.This "second" is another loan which uses the house as collateral but it is often much smaller than the first. While a first mortgage may be for $100,000, a second could be as low as $10,000 or less.

Every time someone takes out a loan, they will have to sign a legally binding contract, which states that the borrower agrees to pay back the loan according to the conditions outlined by the lender.The contract is also called a promissory note and this is where the term "note" comes from. When you purchase a note, you are purchasing someone's loan.

Their obligation to repay that loan will transfer with all of it's terms and conditions to you and you will become the new lender.

Performing vs. Non-Performing

Loans are given to borrowers with the expectation they will be paid back. Most people who take out a loan have every intention of paying back the money they owe.What you'll find as you begin to handle different notes is that a lot of your borrowers have been forced into this situation. Something has happened in their life and they can no longer afford to pay back the loan.

When someone is making monthly payments on their mortgages, these notes are considered to be performing. These loans are basically making the lender money through interest payments and other fees.If the borrower stops paying, for whatever reason, the note will be considered non-performing. At this point, the loan is not making the lender any money and they might want to get rid of it.

A non-performing note is, to put it simply, a loan which someone is not paying back. A non-performing note can be anywhere from a few months late to many years behind in payments.Most banks will hold onto a non-performing note for a while to see if they can work it out. If nothing can be done, however, they often will put these notes up for sale.

Selling the non-performing notes allows them to remove it from their financial records. The selling price of the note will also help the lender make back a portion of the money they've already lost. These notes are generally sold to hedge funds who sometimes will then break them up and sell them to individual investors. Why Would Anyone Buy Them?

The secret to turning something that makes no money into a profitable investment is what we call the "Work-out process". This is the process by which we contact the borrowers and work with them to develop a solution. The reason banks will sell valuable notes is because they don't have the time or inclination to get work-out processes taken care of like I will show you how to do.

The banks simply don't have the time or resources they would need to dedicate to fixing these loans. It's just easier to sell them and be done with the whole ordeal.

Investors like you and me, however, *do* have the time and resources to focus on fixing these notes and that's why this investment works.

Why Juniors?

This book focuses on non-performing junior liens. These are generally second mortgages, which someone took out for one financial reason or another.

In every instance where there is a second mortgage, there will also be a first. This first mortgage may be performing or non-performing, but it will almost always be larger than the second.

Many people have asked me why I stick with junior liens and ignore the seniors.

Logically, the senior lien should be the bigger and more secure investment. Since it is in the first position, there is more control over what can be done with the collateral. When you own a first mortgage you are essentially in command of the fate of this borrower and their house.

While this level of control can be enticing, the drawbacks of investing in senior liens become readily apparent with a little digging.

The first thing to consider is the cost of these notes. A senior lien will likely be a mortgage for a house. This can amount to $500,000 or more in an expensive area of the country.

The first problem with investing in senior liens is that the purchase price can be high for the smaller investor.

You may be able to purchase a non-performing senior lien in a desirable area for about 70 cents on the dollar. This means you could, theoretically, buy a $100,000 senior lien for $70,000.This does leave us with at least $30,000 in profit when all is said and done but we are very tied to this one large investment.

The cost to purchase a loan like this means you might only be able afford to buy a few at a time. Since (on paper) it can take up to 20 or 30 years to make that profit, you can see how limiting senior liens might be.

Junior liens, on the other hand, are often undervalued by the banks and lenders. Since they are in the second position, and therefore don't offer the same level of perceived control as a senior lien, the banks will often price them at a deep discount.

In today's market we can find "quality" non-performing junior liens for about 10 to 30 cents on the dollar.Keep in mind that the total value of these loans will be smaller as well so this means you could purchase a $10,000 loan for about $1,000 to $3,000 dollars.

Potential Profits

This drastic discount in the purchase price causes a few things to happen.

The first is that you'll be able to make a greater potential profit. While we might make $30,000 in profit on our $70,000 investment in the senior lien, we can make a potential $9,000 profit on a $1,000 investment in the junior lien.

This may not sound like a lot but you need look at it in ratios and capital risk analysis. The return on investment percentage you'll make from a junior lien is much higher than what you could make from a senior lien.

With a junior lien, however, your profit could be 100% or more of the investment cost. When you extrapolate these numbers to account for multiple notes, you can see how junior liens might allow you to multiply your money many times over.

Risk Factor

The other result of this discounted purchase price is a decrease in the overall risk of this investment strategy. Non-performing senior liens can be quite expensive and will represent a rather large investment.

The amount of money tied up into one of these notes is large enough that you will always be concerned with making it work.

If you don't make a profit from that one single note, you can potentially lose quite a bit of money. That's a lot of eggs in one basket.

The cost of investing in junior liens is so much lower that we could purchase many junior liens for the price of one senior lien.

You could, in some cases, purchase a very large number of junior liens for the same price you would pay for just one senior lien. What this allows you to do is *"hedge your bets"*.

Here is a great example I always like to use...

Let's say you're heading to a casino and you have a $100 bankroll. There are plenty of different games to bet on but you want to make as much money as possible.

One option would be to go to the roulette table and put all of your money on black (one big bet).It's a 50/50 chance and you could either double your money or walk away broke. This is a gamble which could either pay off well or leave you feeling a little empty.

Another option would be to head over to the blackjack table. Here you'll be able to place bets on 20 different hands at $5 each.

You may lose a couple of hands along the way but, when you do, you're only losing $5 each time. You will also, however, win a few hands and this success can end up covering all of your losses.

When the game is over, you'll be walking away with a nice potential profit (making many smaller bets).

The money you make playing blackjack may not be as much as what you could potentially win by playing roulette but there is much less risk associated with it.

By breaking up your bankroll into 20 smaller increments, you were able to spend it in such a way that success has a stronger chance if you sharpen your skills at the game of blackjack. You've hedged your bets and this is exactly what you might be doing with notes.

Purchasing these lower priced notes allows us to buy enough of them that we can spread our risks. There is no need to be overly concerned with any one note because we will have a handful of other notes which can also make us a nice potential profit.

In addition to this, we will have less money tied up in these investments.

Notes vs. Real Estate investing

Notes can be created for nearly anything but this book will focus on those notes which use physical properties as collateral.

Many people mistake notes for a real estate investment. While I have invested in real estate for many years, I personally believe notes are a better option for short term cash flow and I'll explain why.

Investing in real estate can be a great way to make money. It's a high-value market and well located, desirable real estate is always in demand, even if the markets fluctuate periodically.

One problem with real estate, however, is the amount of hands on effort associated with much of it. When you invest in real estate, you are buying a house and then renting it out.

When you do this, you've become the landlord. Since you own the house, you're responsible for things like taxes, repairs, and continued maintenance.

Different things will go wrong with a house on a regular basis. Small things such as plumbing and wiring problems will pop up all the time.

Major things, such as needing to replace the roof or air conditioning, are inevitable. All of this represents quite a lot of time and money and this can make investing in real estate difficult. It can be a lot of responsibility—or in other words, *stress.*

What makes notes different from real estate is that you aren't buying the responsibility for a property. You have only purchased a loan for which the house is collateral and not the house itself.

Your borrower will still own their home and will be responsible for all of the continuing repairs and maintenance which the house might require.

This makes notes a relatively passive investment. Once you have completed the work-out stage and have gotten the note to begin performing again, there is very little for you to do.

The only real work required by a fixed note is regular bookkeeping and a monthly trip to the bank. You won't have to worry about anything relating to the house in any way.

Another difference is that of location. Real estate investors are generally told to purchase properties close to where they live. Since the condition of the property is so important, it can be a good idea to keep it close enough that regular visits can be made.

With notes, however, you won't ever need to visit the property, which means you are more free to invest in notes which are tied to properties all over the country.

These notes will be tied to a great variety of different properties. If you were a real estate investor and wanted to invest in a $500,000 home, then you would need to pay about $500,000.Junior liens, as you'll find, can actually be tied to houses of differing values.

You could, for example, pay $5,000 for a $50,000 junior lien note and find it is for a house with a fair market value of $300,000. By investing in junior liens, you'll be able to create a diverse portfolio made up of notes tied to properties of all kinds.

The Hidden Gold Mine

Notes have been my preferred investment for a number of years now. When I first started purchasing them, I had a lot to learn. There were many fears which hung around in the back of my mind, causing me to doubt my strategies.

As I gained more experience, however, I began to find that many of my fears were not only unfounded but could be used to my benefit in one way or another.

This is one of the reasons I think notes are the best investments available today. There are far too many investment strategies which require a close adherence to a certain process. Things can only be done one way and there is no room for creativity.

Notes are great because they offer plenty of space to begin tweaking and customizing the basic strategies outlined in this book.

Essentially, however, I have chosen notes for some very basic reasons. The first is the amount of money needed to start investing in them. As I've already said, junior liens are much more affordable than senior liens.

The cost to purchase a junior lien is so low, in fact, that nearly everyone can afford to purchase one. Investments like real estate and even company stocks can end up costing tens, or even hundreds of thousands of dollars. A non-performing junior lien might only cost a few thousand.

This opens the world of investing to a much larger group of people. These are investments with a huge potential for profit and they only require a small amount of money to purchase.

Rather than spending all of your life savings on one big, risky investment, you can purchase a bunch of non-performing junior liens and potentially make just as much money, if not more.

Simply put, there are very few other investments which can currently offer an exponential return on the investment cost. The upside to these loans might outweigh the risk you might have to take on when you buy them.

Don't get me wrong...there is risk associated with these notes. You have to keep in mind that these are delinquent loans, which means the borrower has not been paying them back for quite a long time.

In any one instance, you are taking on quite a lot of risk. Since these notes are so affordable, however, you can purchase a great number of them which allows you to hedge your bets and reduce the overall risk.

For every additional note you purchase, you're decreasing the chances of losing all of your money. Since this book will focus on purchasing multiple non-performing junior liens, you will be learning about an investment strategy which actually has a surprisingly low amount of risk.

When you combine the low purchase price and the high profit margin with the ability to mitigate risk, it's fairly easy to see why I've made non-performing junior liens such a major part of my financial life.

Over the course of this book I will explain everything in detail. I will point out common problems and offer some useful suggestions for overcoming them.

By the time you're done, you will have all of the knowledge needed to not only begin investing in notes but to excel at it. This book has been written with the individual, average investor in mind. What you're reading right now is a road map to the type of success I've been enjoying doing exactly what is outlined in the coming pages.

CHAPTER THREE:

Opportunities and the Current Market

Before I go into the details of how a profit can be made from non-performing junior liens, I feel it's important to take a look at the current market and determine the opportunities available in it.

Our current financial market is in the middle of a recovery period. Just like someone convalescing from a major injury, it's taken a few years before any improvement has been seen.

People all over the country are still worried. The fall of the housing market has had far-reaching consequences and has affected nearly every area of the economy.

Many people have lost a lot of money, businesses have closed down, and homes have been foreclosed on in staggering numbers. All of this has led to rampant uncertainty and fear.

The fact is, many people are afraid because they don't know what is going to happen. They don't want to invest because the markets have been so volatile. There is a rule in business, however, which states that uncertainty is evidence of opportunity and this is never more true than in the non-performing note market.

Uncertainty, in fact, is what non performing notes are all about. These are loans which had been created by a bank, loans which then fell apart.

The banks simply aren't set up to fix these notes and they have let them remain delinquent for many months or even years in some cases.

The borrowers are also mired in uncertainty because they know they're behind on their loans but they have no idea what is going to happen to them, their family, or their home.

What we offer as note investors is an end to this uncertainty. When we purchase these notes, the banks have found their solution and no longer need to worry about the note.

When we begin working with the borrowers, we start removing their uncertainty as well. Once the process is finished, they will know exactly how much they need to pay and will no longer need to worry about being evicted from their home.

Your Chance to Fix It

This is where our profit really comes from. You make money on a note because you're able to fix it. One thing many people don't understand is that banks are simply loan originators.

Their entire job is to create loans and make a profit from the interest payments. What they aren't set up to do, however, is handle these loans when they fall apart.

As you read through this book, you'll begin to realize there is a process to fixing a delinquent note. While this process is not exactly complicated, it can take time, money, and a certain amount of effort, diligence and patience.

More importantly, fixing a note really requires *close personal attention*. Our strategy works because we're able to work directly with the borrower one-one-one over time. Banks just do not have the time or resources to do this.

When a bank originates a loan, it will place a certain value on that note and add it to their portfolio. If the loan stops performing, the value will begin to drop.

Once it has been delinquent for a number of months, most banks will drop the value of the note to zero. It is not making them any money and therefore is not worth much to them.

Many banks today, will have a large collection of these non-performing notes and they want to get rid of them. When they sell their notes to you or a hedge fund, the money made from the sale actually shows up as a profit in their financial reports.

This means they've actually managed to make some money from the loan, money which they can use to originate more reliable loans.

The Current Glut

Ordinarily, most banks will not have too many delinquent loans on their books. Every lender has a certain process by which they weed out unreliable prospective borrowers.

People who want to take out a loan will have to qualify for it and prove they can pay it back, plus interest. This is the traditional method of creating reliable and profitable loans but it is not what was being done during the past decade.

Starting sometime around 2004 and ending when the

bubble burst in 2008, banks and lenders all over the country were creating a lot of loans. At first, this seemed like a great boon to the financial industry as well as the real estate market.

There were suddenly legions of people with tons of money in their pocket and they wanted to invest in high value properties.

The problem, however, was that many of these people didn't actually qualify for the loans they were receiving. Banks and lenders had essentially done away with the qualification process which had been used to create secure loans in the past.

Many of these people were risky borrowers and so the banks decided to mitigate that risk with variable interest rates and weak underwriting.

Things went fine for a few years, while the bubble was still growing, but it all began to fall apart like a tower made of dominoes. As the bubble reached its peak, people began losing money on their investments. Property values were dropping and the banks started to get scared.

During this period of time, the country saw an unprecedented period of loan creation. Banks were creating more loans than ever and were giving them to people who didn't really qualify.

As the bubble burst, record numbers of these loans went delinquent and the banks were inundated with loans that were in limbo.

Not only are banks not normally set up to fix delinquent loans, they had far more of them than they could ever hope to deal with.

The inventory of non-performing liens began to grow ever more abundant until the banks were forced to sell off large pools of these notes in an effort to make back some of their money. Hedge funds were their primary customers and these notes then entered the market.

What this means for you is there is a huge abundance of these non-performing notes and more are entering the market every day. There are, in fact, still many notes which have yet to be sold.

These notes are sitting in a bank vault, accruing late fees and missed payments but never once being touched by the bank itself. These notes will also enter the market as they're sold off.

How Long Will it Last?

What we have right now is a market which is full of these non-performing notes. Not every one of them is a junior lien but there are quite a few and many more which have yet to be sold by the banks.

In fact...over the next few years, the number of non-performing junior liens which are in the market will continue to grow, whether they're up for sale or in the process of being worked out.

As this happens, we'll see countless new opportunities spring up and will be able to search these inventories for those notes which fit perfectly into the strategy outlined in this book.

But, this situation won't last forever. The banks have started tightening their qualification requirements and haven't been originating as many loans as they were only a few years ago.

While a few of these recent loans may eventually stop performing and end up for sale, there will be far fewer notes for us in the future.

How long this period of abundance will last is hard to predict, but I feel it's safe to say we will have this current opportunity for the next two to three years.

This means there is a limited amount of time during which you can take full advantage of the opportunities available in this junior lien niche with today's high inventory and at todays prices.

While there is currently a great abundance of non-performing notes, the large inventory will eventually run out. Will there always be non-performing junior liens? – absolutely – but the current glut of opportunity makes this time unique in my opinion.

Not All Notes are the Same

Investors like myself have recently seen a huge surge in the number of non-performing notes entering the market. What you'll realize as you learn more about it, however, is that we have a rather specific set of criteria for the notes we purchase.

The strategy outlined in this book is focused on one particular type of note. This is the non-performing junior lien, tied to an owner occupied primary residence.

If you apply this criteria to the current inventory of notes, you'll find the numbers begin to shrink. The problem is that banks are selling off all sorts of notes.

Some of them are senior liens, some juniors, and some have nothing to do with real estate at all. A lot of these notes are also for properties which may never turn around in our life time.

Some states were hit harder than others when the bubble burst. Cities like Detroit have been damaged so badly that it may be a lost cause for now, at least as far as we're concerned. These houses may have once been desirable but are now located in nearly abandoned, crime ridden neighborhoods.

To make matters worse, many of these properties have been unoccupied for a number of years.

These houses have not been taken care of and are falling apart. Since they are located in such awful neighborhoods, many of them have been occupied by squatters and drug dealers or have simply been stripped of their copper pipes and wiring and left to rot.

Houses like these need to be avoided at all costs. There is simply no way to make money from them in our current economy.

The notes tied to these properties are so far outside of my criteria, in fact, that I would assign them a negative value. These notes are such a bad investment that someone would have to actually pay me money to take possession of them.

They may be priced incredibly low, but that is money I will simply lose because there is no way to make a profit from them. The only way you could make money with one of these notes is if the seller paid you to buy them.

When you consider these facts, you can see how the current inventory is not as large as it might appear. Many of the notes which are either up for sale now or will be sold in the near future do not fit into my investment strategy.

Instead of having thousands of notes to choose from, I may only have a few hundred at any one time. Since these will fit into my criteria, however, there is plenty of opportunity for profit.

The Time is Now

All of this is, in a roundabout way, telling you that if you are interested, *now is the time* to start investing in non-performing junior liens.

There are plenty of notes to choose from and there are still more waiting to enter into the market. The banks still have piles of these notes in their vaults and they will be selling them off in large pools as time goes on.

These notes can be long term investments, if that's what you want. They're available now and you can hold onto them for decades.

Even though you can collect profits from these notes for years to come, you won't be able to buy them at today's prices for long. These ideal notes are limited and they will eventually be gone.

New notes will always pop up, but it will never happen in the numbers we're seeing today—at least until the next market cycle.

If you're reading this book, then you're probably interested in notes. The best advice I can give you is to read through this book, absorb the information, and then begin buying your own notes right away.

CHAPTER FOUR:

How and Why it Works

Logically speaking, it shouldn't make sense that we can generate so much money from a debt which someone has stopped paying on. These are loans which haven't made their lenders any money for months or years.

The first obstacle I face, when teaching people about this investment, is helping them to understand a few important concepts. These concepts are the key to why investing in non-performing junior liens works.

Financial vs. Emotional Equity

The first concept you need to understand is the frame of mind of most home buyers. It can be far too easy to view all real estate as an investment.

The only reason an investor purchases a house is to make money from it. He is not planning on living in it and is only concerned with the condition and location of the house because those will determine the amount of money he can make.

Most people, however, will not buy a house as an investment. While selling their home may be in the back of their mind, they don't plan to do that for many years.

When people buy a house, they're looking for a home. They aren't concerned with the money they will make when they sell it. They're only interested in whether or not the house will make a good home for their family.

A house becomes a home rather quickly. The family will move in, get comfortable, and eventually become a part of the local community.

Their kids will attend the school, they may join the local church, and they will begin to make friends with the neighbors. All of this is stuff which cannot be quantified by a financial figure. You just can't put a price on a home.

This is what I call "Emotional Equity". As a real estate investor, you would be worried about the financial equity in the home.

The homebuyer who took out the loan we're purchasing, however, is only concerned with the emotional equity they've built up in their home.

The longer they've lived there, the more emotional equity there will be. Simply put, the presence of emotional equity means the homeowner does not want to leave.

When there is emotional equity in place, the homeowner's greatest fear is being foreclosed on and losing their home. They will be forced out and will need to uproot their family, severing all of the connections they've made over the years.

The money lost when they're foreclosed on is of little concerned when compared with the possibility of losing their home and the life they've built.

Humans vs. Institutions

Emotional equity is important and it's what you will leverage when working with the borrower. The process of working with them, however, is what really makes you a profit.

After you purchase a note, you will then contact the borrower and try to come up with a mutually beneficial solution. You can modify the loan so it fits into their budget and the homeowner will be happy to agree to it because it helps them stay in their home.

The fact that you can actually work with the borrower is what sets you apart from the banks. When someone stops paying off a loan, the bank will do what it can to get them to start paying again.

The problem is there isn't much a bank can do. They can send letters and make phones calls but the only powerful tool in their arsenal is foreclosure.

And as I mentioned before, banks don't have the time or resources to begin working with a borrower.

More importantly, these lenders are not very interested in modifying the loan in any way. When a bank originates a $100,000 loan, for example, it has essentially cost them $100,000.If they modify the loan they would potentially lose money which would ruin the value of the bank as a business.

As a note investor, on the other hand, you've purchased the note at an incredible discount. Non-performing junior lien notes can, in fact, be purchased for as little as 10% of the total value of the loan.

Since you can buy a $100,000 loan for only $10,000, there is plenty of room to work with the borrower. Any dollar you receive past that $10,000 purchase price is profit.

This allows you to work closely with the borrower, determine the extent of their financial resources, and then create a new payment plan which they will be able to follow without any trouble. This is something the banks not only can't do but wouldn't do even if they had the chance.

A New Sheriff

As an actual human, and not an institution, you can focus your own personal attention on a note. Many of these notes have been dormant for years.

They haven't been paid in a long time and many of the borrowers may have either forgotten about the loan or are hoping it has just disappeared. The borrowers think they can continue to dodge the bank until it gives up and never pay back the loan.

One of the most important reasons this investment works is the way we change the game by purchasing a note.

Until you've bought it, the borrower hasn't had anyone attempt to really solve this problem and has chosen to just ignore it.The first step, after purchasing the note, is to begin contacting the borrower and explaining to them that you are a real human and intend to fix this note, one way or another.

Your borrower has more than likely become rather comfortable with the idea of never paying off this note. They've lived their lives for years, never really thinking about their loan and are often no longer concerned about someone coming after them.

Needless to say, this first contact is often a big shock. They're suddenly faced with a situation where someone is personally working on their loan and will to do whatever it takes to get the loan paid off.

All of the sudden, foreclosure is back on the table and there is nowhere to run. You're on the case and you will not let them slip away again.

While the bank may have left the note to rot in the vault, you are going to diligently work on it, every day, until the note either starts performing or is paid off through a short sale or foreclosure.

Relationship Building

While this can be a shock to your borrowers, you will approach them in a friendly and helpful manner.

The truth is, your goals are the same as your borrower's goals. You both want them to stay in their house and you both want this loan to be paid off. The best way to achieve a mutually beneficial solution is to build a relationship with your borrower.

One of the most important parts of any successful note investment is the beginning of the Work-out process. During this time, you will simply be gathering information and getting to know your borrower.

You'll be learning about them, understanding them on a deeply personal level and beginning to get into their frame of mind.

This is really the major difference between you and a bank. A bank doesn't care about the borrower on a personal level. They only care about their bottom line.

Unlike an employee, you care more about the borrower because your borrower is the one who will be making *you* a personal profit. This, in turn, makes the borrower much more interested in working with you.

The success of any particular note depends on your relationship with the borrower more than any other factor in this business. Your personal relationship is what makes all the difference and without it, there can be no solution.

Since banks are never interested in personal relationships of any kind, it's easy to see why they're having so much trouble fixing these delinquent loans.

An Ongoing Relationship

The relationship you build with your borrowers is meant to last a long time. It will exist throughout the life of the loan and will continue to create a profitable investment as the years go on.

Many of these loans might last for decades and there are a countless number of problems which might arise. Borrowers can get injured, lose their job or run into other unexpected financial burdens.

At this point, they may not be able to continue following the payment plan until they get back on their feet. Since you've built a high level of respect with this person, they won't simply stop paying.

It's important to let the borrowers know that they should contact you if they run into any problems which might cause them to stop sending payments each month.

They'll do this for two reasons:

The first is that they know your loan servicer will initiate foreclosure immediately and it can be a costly and frustrating process for everyone involved.

The second reason is that they trust and like you because you were the only one who helped them through one of the toughest periods of their lives.

Simply put, they know you will help them through this most recent struggle as well.

This is not something they will get from a bank. Even if the borrower was able to luck out and find a bank employee that can help them, they will probably not be working with that person again.

If this problem arises ten years down the line, that person may have been fired, promoted, or reassigned to another department. When the borrower calls their bank, they will be speaking with someone new almost every time.

Worse yet, the person they're talking to will probably not have the power or authority to do anything helpful. The only thing they're allowed to do is demand payment, label the loan as delinquent, and eventually send it through the system to be foreclosed on.

This bank employee will not be able to create a temporary modification which might see the borrower through a storm.

The Freedom to Be Creative

Every note you purchase is yours and you can do whatever you like with it. You have the freedom to reduce the principle, waive the arrears, lower the interest rate, extended the length of the loan or make any other changes which can help make a loan start performing again.

More importantly, you have the freedom to do it again. If your borrower contacts you and explains the situation, you can modify the loan again so they will be able to continue paying it off.

You might have to reduce the monthly payments for a short period of time but the important thing is that you're able to do that. Banks and bank employees simply can't.

All of this modification works because your borrower has come to trust you and believes you are looking out for their best interest. It may take some time to get to this point but your relationship with them is the most powerful tool available to you.

This relationship is what will cause them to work with you, it's what will make them call you if any problems come up in the future.

This gives you the freedom to be in control of your investments. The entire work-out process happens between you and the borrower and no one else. This is a one-on-one, high touch, incredibly personal business.

The freedom you have allows you do things the banks can't. More importantly, you can do them faster, easier, and with less cost.

This is why investing in non-performing junior liens works so well.

CHAPTER FIVE:

Finding and Purchasing the Notes

The most important thing to do, before you can begin investing in notes, is to learn where to find them and what to look for.

Non-performing notes come in a number of different forms. While this book will focus on notes attached to real estate, they can represent loans for nearly anything you can think of.

No matter what they may be for, the notes we purchase will generally follow the same life cycle. They are created, sold, and acquired in the same way in nearly every instance.

Understanding this life cycle can give you a unique perspective into the reasons we buy these notes, and it will offer some insight into why they can be so profitable.

The Life Cycle of a Non-Performing Real Estate Note

Every real estate note starts life in the same way. Each begins with a person's dream to buy a house. This person has been saving up their money, researching different properties and has eventually chosen the home in which they want to live.

Generally speaking, however, most people do not have the money to purchase a home outright. More often than not, someone will go to a bank or other lending institution and apply for a loan.

A Note is Created

The loan process will vary from one lender to another. The person who is requesting the loan will go to the bank and present a variety of financial information.

This paperwork focuses on the person's own finances and is designed to ensure they have the resources needed to pay back the loan. The bank will check things such as credit reports, income, and expenses to determine if the loan payments fall into an acceptable range.

Once the loan is approved, the borrower signs the loan agreement. This agreement will outline the amount of the loan, the amount of time the borrower has to repay the loan, and the expected monthly payments as well as the interest rate.

This agreement is a promissory note and it's a legally binding contract between the borrower and the lender.

There will often be some fine print within the loan agreement. This will cover things like penalties for late payments and the consequences for nonpayment.

Most people are honest and hardworking, and when they take out a loan they have every intention of paying it back. Many of these loans, however, will last for 20 or 30 years and a variety of things can happen in that time.

The Note Stops Performing

One of the most common misconceptions about non-performing real estate notes is that the borrowers associated with these notes are untrustworthy.

The simple truth is no one can predict what will happen in the next 10 or 20 years. In many cases, things were going well and the borrower was diligently making payments until they ran into some sort of financial hardship. This could be a loss of income, unexpected repairs, or even medical expenses.

Most people live on a rather tight budget and there is not much room for large expenses such as hospital stays. Even if the person has never broken an agreement in their life, there is a chance they'll be faced with a situation where they can no longer afford the monthly payments on their mortgage.

Since we are dealing with junior liens, which are second mortgages, the borrower will often choose to keep paying their first mortgage but will neglect the second.

Notes will usually offer some sort of grace period. While late payments will always incur penalties, the loan will not default until a certain number of months have gone by without a payment.

Once this happens, however, the note is considered to be non-performing and something must be done.

The first step is to contact the borrower and inform them of the situation. If they honestly can't make payments anymore, the bank will need to take action and try to recover their losses.

The Note is Sold

Nearly every bank and lending institution will have a department that deals with non-performing notes. These are loans the bank issued that have stopped performing— meaning the borrower is not making any payments.

There is, in fact, one person whose job it is to clear all of these non-performing notes from the bank's ledger.

The reason for this is that banks make money by issuing loans. When they give someone a loan, they will expect monthly payments with interest.

Over time, this interest begins to turn a profit. When the loan is completely paid off, the bank will have made a healthy profit while at the same time collecting back all of the money they loaned out.

When a note stops performing, however, the bank is losing money. Not only are they not making a profit from the interest but they are not making back the initial money they gave to the borrower. .

They face a problem because they only have two options when it comes to recovering this lost capital.

The first option is to foreclose on the house. This requires the bank to take possession of the house and then sell it (often at a reduced price) in an effort to mitigate some of their losses.

The problem with foreclosure is that it can be a lengthy and laborious process. When you consider the fact that a bank might have hundreds, or even thousands, of these defaulted loans, it's easy to see why they would not want to foreclose in every instance.

The other option is to sell the note to someone who purchases non-performing notes—or, in our case, non-performing junior liens. They will often sell it for much less than the full value of the loan. But by selling it, the bank will recover some of the money it lost.

More importantly for them, it can finally remove these delinquent loans from its ledger. Sometimes banks aren't allowed to make as many new loans until enough bad ones are off the books.

The Note is Purchased

This is how a note will enter into the market and become available for sale. This is not, however, the level at which we usually purchase the note.

As I mentioned before, banks will often have a huge collection of these non-performing notes and they will want to get rid of them as quickly and easily as possible.

Rather than selling each note by itself, they will bundle them together into what is called a "pool" of notes.

This pool can vary in size but will always consist of loans issued by the bank. The bank's reputation is tied to these loans and they are very picky about who they deal with.

What this means for us is that most banks will not want to deal with you as an individual investor.

They want to sell a large package of notes to someone who they know will handle them correctly and within the legalities of the mortgage lending industry as borrowers remember who they originally got the loan from.

Most individual note investors will not purchase directly from the bank. While this may sometimes be possible, the primary purchaser at this level will be hedge funds.

A hedge fund is a group of investors who have pooled their money together in an effort to invest in something rather expensive.

The hedge fund will approach the bank and ask to see the notes available for purchase. They will analyze each pool according to very specific criteria and will eventually choose one to buy.

Once they have purchased these notes, they have now traded places with the bank. The hedge fund is, legally speaking, the lender and all of the borrower's obligations to repay the loan are transferred to them.

At this point, the hedge fund can attempt to work with the borrowers and get them to start paying again.

Since they have purchased so many notes, however, getting each one to start performing again could be a monstrous task. The faster and more profitable option at this level is to start selling the notes to other investors.

The Note is Sold Again

What most hedge funds do is they will look at the pool of notes they have purchased. There will likely be an assortment of good notes and bad notes—meaning there are some with a potential to become performing again and some which are a lot less likely.

The hedge fund will then break apart their pool of notes and create a collection of smaller pools.

These smaller pools are then put up for sale to other investors. These investors are often smaller hedge funds which are looking for a slightly more affordable investment.

The cost of the pools will be marginally higher than what they were initially purchased for. Selling them this way gives the original hedge fund the ability to make a nice profit in a short period of time.

Depending on the size of the pools at this point, the smaller hedge funds may do the same thing. This cycle may, in fact, be repeated a number of times.

Larger pools will be purchased, broken up into smaller pools, sold and then broken up and sold again. Each step in this process makes the pools of notes smaller and more affordable while only eroding a small fraction of their potential value.

Individuals Purchase the Note

This is the point in the process where individual investors will enter the scene. Once the smaller hedge funds have sorted through their notes, they will often put them up for sale.

At this level, the notes may either be sold in very small pools or as individual notes. A variety of information is posted about each note and you will be able to determine a bit about the value of the loan and the location of the property.

Once an individual has purchased a note, there are a number steps they can take. These can include things such as working with the borrower to get the note performing as well as selling the note yet again.

Turning a non-performing note back into a performing note is the best way to make the most money from this type of investment. This technique will be covered in the coming chapters.

Ordinarily, most investors would not want to be at the end of a supply chain. When a business purchases a product, for example, they will get the best price when the product is purchased directly from the manufacturer.

The cost of this product will generally increase when multiple distributors are added into the process. Notes, however, are different.

Being able to purchase individual notes has a few key benefits. The greatest benefit is the ability to pick and choose which notes you want.

When these notes are sold as pools, you are required many times to either purchase the entire pool or nothing at all in a competitive bidding process. There is no way to pick out the good ones and avoid the bad ones.

When buying them individually, on the other hand, you can purchase only those notes which best fit with your strategy.

More importantly, the greatest profit potential is found at the end of the line. When a hedge fund purchases a pool of notes, they will generally not be interested in working with the borrower.

Their whole business models centers on simply reselling these notes at a slight mark up. A note may, for example, initially enter the market for $5,000. By the time it reaches the individual investors, the cost may be about $7,000 or more.

What you have to remember, however, is the ultimate value of this loan could be $50,000 or even much more. This means the loan, if it was made to re-perform and was eventually paid off completely, would earn the note holder the full $50,000 plus any interest and late fees which might have accrued over time.

Simply put, the return on the investment is much higher at this point in the process than at any other.

Buying the Best Notes

In the world of note pool buying, there is a saying which goes: "Always avoid the bottom third."

This refers to the nature of notes and the way in which the pools are created. Notes can generally be broken up into three different categories.

These are:

- **Top Quality Notes**

  These are notes which carry very little risk. The borrower is trustworthy, there is equity in place and the likelihood of a successful work out is high.

  These notes are somewhat rare and will generally cost more money.

- **Mid-Level Notes**

These are the most common type of notes. The risks and rewards may be about even. There may be some small amount of equity or some other factor which leans more towards success than failure.

These notes will generally be more affordable.

- **Bad Notes (The Bottom Third)**

  These notes are the bottom of the barrel. The risks may far outweigh the potential for rewards. Some of these notes have been non-performing for a long time or are tied to extremely undesirable collateral.

  In terms of an investment, not much should be paid for these quality of notes.

When pools of are created, they can contain notes from any of these categories. Many hedge funds, however, will create pools which are heavier on one type of note than another.

There might be pools with a large number of high quality notes while others may consist mostly of low grade, weaker investments.

My goal has been to develop a *relationships* with these sellers. I wanted more than a working relationship. I needed to develop a level of trust and confidence which would prove to them that I could handle their notes.

Reputations are on the line and the people who sell these notes are very selective when it comes to who they will deal with.

I also wanted to make sure I could trust them. Since I planned on investing a significant amount of money, I had to be absolutely sure I was getting the best quality notes at the best price I could find.

This relationship-building accounted for a lot of time but, in the end, I was left with a small group of note vendors with whom I had built a relationship based on trust and follow through of commitments.

This, of course, does not mean I expect you to travel the country, taking note vendors out to lunch. I simply want to illustrate how personal this business can be.

Personal relationships are what create success at every step in the process. The sooner you start building them, the quicker you will start seeing profits.

Considerations

Now that you understand a bit about how notes are created and where they come from, there are a few important considerations to keep in mind. There will be a good deal of information to look at with each note.

This information will help determine if the note is a good investment or if it should be avoided in favor of something better. The following are a few general things to keep in mind before searching for your first note.

Pools vs. Individual Notes

As an investor, you will have the option of purchasing either individual notes or entire pools. These pools can range in size depending on where and how they are purchased. Some pools will have *hundreds* of different notes while others may contain only a few.

Deciding on whether to purchase single or multiple notes can be a bit tricky at first and is really a matter of personal taste.

Neither option is fundamentally better than the other but there are a few things to keep in mind. The most obvious consideration is that of price. A pool of notes will almost always cost more than any individual note.

This higher dollar amount will sometimes keep

individual investors from being able to purchase entire pools. In other cases, purchasing pools may not fit in with your investment strategy.

Another factor is that of quality. Every note is different and some will be better than others. When I talk about the quality of the note, I'm referring to a few different things.

The most important in analyzing a junior lien is whether or not the borrower is a good re-performance risk. Since we are going to be making the majority of our money by working with the borrower, I want to make sure they will work with us.

Pools, however, might consist of both high and low quality notes. When purchased together, the quality may be diverse enough so as to balance out the risks and rewards.

Rehabilitating these lower quality notes may, however, take a bit more time, effort and money and so they can often be troublesome for someone new to this market.

As we have said, purchasing individual notes allows you to choose the best ones. You will be able to go through the available information and pick out only those notes with the best profit potential.

This might mean you will be purchasing far fewer notes, but the ones you do buy will be of the highest possible quality.

Location

While investing in notes may share some similarities with investing in physical real estate, there are a few key differences and one of them is location. Most people who invest in real estate are taught to look for properties in their own neighborhood.

The idea is to only purchase properties within a close proximity to where the investor lives.

The reason for this is simple. Someone who owns physical property will want to inspect it from time to time. They will also be responsible for both regular maintenance and any unexpected repairs which need to be done.

In addition, most people are experts when it comes to their own home town and they will be able to find the best investment properties with only a little research.

Notes, however, are not really a real estate investment. What we mean by this is that you're not purchasing physical property—just the loan which was used to purchase that property.

You are not responsible for repairs or maintenance and do not really need to worry about the property or the house at all.

When purchasing discounted non-performing notes for a very low investment and no plans to foreclose, than location becomes a much smaller piece of the equation.

This does not mean you will never be able to find notes which are tied to properties in your home town, but they will likely be rare. Most notes are created by banks and large lending institutions.

Some of these banks will be familiar names such as Wells Fargo and Citibank. These are national (or sometimes international) chains, which means their notes will be located all over the country.

Cost

The cost of a note will vary greatly depending on a few different factors. As an investor, this means you will be able to find notes which fit perfectly into your budget.

Generally speaking, however, the quality of a note is what really determines its price. There are plenty of non-performing notes which are incredibly cheap but the likelihood of successfully rehabilitating them is low.

Fortunately, this type investing has a much lower cost of entry than real estate investing.

The initial investment we usually suggest is somewhere around $50,000 because this is enough to purchase a few different notes while still allowing you to choose those notes with a healthy potential for profit.

The most important consideration when it comes to cost is your overall resources. I always tell people not to invest their "lunch" money. This should not be money on which you need to live. Things can sometimes go wrong, and some money can be lost.

But the biggest reason is that these notes will often take a few years to realize their full value. You may be holding onto a note for 5 or even 10 years, during which time the investment capital will be tied up.

The bottom line is that you do not want to go broke purchasing your first few notes. You will need to create a budget which will support your investment strategy while allowing you to continue to live your life.

You need to have enough money left over to keep paying your bills. This is why we always suggest investing only as much as you can afford.

Evaluating Notes

There are a few different ways to evaluate a note and this should be done before any of them are purchased. This is one of the most important steps in the process and you need to learn what to look for and what to avoid.

Most of these are relatively simple. They will become

more familiar and obvious as you gain experience in the field.

When you first begin looking at the available notes, you will have access to a variety of information. Most of this will not pertain to the borrower but will focus mainly on the loan itself.

You will see certain things such as the originator of the loan, its unpaid principal balance, and the amount of time and debt which is left.

Here are a few brief things which you should keep in mind when choosing a note:

❖ **How many times has it been sold?**

> Due to the way in which notes are bought and sold, any given note may have passed through a number of different hands.

❖ **How long has the loan been delinquent?**

> When a borrower defaults on their loan, that note may not be sold immediately. Since banks will usually package all of their delinquent loans together, it may take some time before that pool is created and sold.
> In general, the longer a loan has been delinquent, the harder it might be to rehabilitate it.
> A loan which has been delinquent for a long time, however, will often have quite a few penalties and late fees, which can actually increase our final profit.

❖ **Is it a senior or junior lien?**

> Both junior and senior liens have a different list of acquisition and due diligence considerations,

problems and goals.

❖ Who is selling the note?

This is a very important piece of information and it will often have very little to do with any individual note. There are plenty of different places from which to purchase notes and each seller will be different.

You want to make sure you are making the best possible investments so you want to buy from a reputable and trusted seller.

❖ How much is left on the loan?

Depending on the note, some of the principle may have already been paid off. Some of these notes will have been performing for a few years before the borrower stopped paying.

It is important to determine how much money is left before the loan is paid off—including any fees or penalties—because this will help determine how much profit can be made from that note.

Evaluating the Borrower

When you invest in real estate, the most important thing to look into is the property. Real estate investors want to make sure they are buying a property which has been well maintained and is up-to-date.

With non-performing notes, however, we are far less concerned with the house than with the borrower. As far as we are concerned, the house is simply the collateral on the loan.

For us, the borrower is the most important factor. The reason for this is the borrower will be producing the profit we make from our investments.

Since we are purchasing notes with the intention of rehabilitating them, we want to make sure we are purchasing loans which are attached to low risk borrowers.

The problem we face, however, is that we are not allowed to contact the borrower in any way prior to purchase of the notes.

When you go to look at the notes available for sale, you will have to sign what is called a non-complete non-disclosure agreement (NDNA). This agreement is to protect the borrower and it bars you from contacting them until the purchase is complete.

Credit Reports

Fortunately, there is a way around this roadblock. We can actually learn quite a lot about a borrower by taking a look at their credit report. This will give us some insight into what their financial situation is like.

What we are looking for is a willingness to repay their loan and enough assets and income to do so.

One warning flag in a credit report is excessive debt. While there are a variety of different types of debt, they will all put a strain on the borrower.

When someone has more debt than they can handle, they will often file for bankruptcy, which can cause us a few problems as investors. The presence of other debt also means there are fewer available resources to work with—meaning less cash to pay *you*.

Another thing we always look for is a history of failure to repay debts or carry out obligations.

A credit report might show, for example, that this person has repeatedly missed payments or outright refused to repay a loan.

Other things, such as a failure to pay child support can say a lot about the character of the borrower and what it will be like to work with them.

Many people will fall behind on their mortgage payments through no real fault of their own. They may have lost their job or run into unexpected medical bills. These people will have a relatively clean credit history and have always paid their debts on time.

Although this person may currently be in a tough financial spot, they would be more than willing to pay back the note if they could. This is our ideal borrower.

Ordinarily, we would need the borrower's permission to pull their credit report. Since I'm not allowed to contact the borrower, I get it from the entity selling the note. They will usually have pulled the same credit file within the last six months.

Equity and Emotional Equity

Equity is a simple concept and is one of the most important factors in real estate investing. Every house has a value which is determined by the market.

If we sell this house, we still need to pay anything which is left on the mortgage. The amount of money left over after we pay off the lien is the equity.

Here is an example:

$100,000 House
- $75,000 Mortgage

$25,000 Equity

While financial equity is an important consideration, we are not interested in owning the house. The truth is, as an investor in junior liens, you will rarely, if ever, need to be concerned with foreclosing on the home.

Since we want the borrower to start repaying the loan, what we are really interested in is the "emotional" equity.

Emotional equity is a concept we have developed which can help you understand why this investment works. When we look for notes, we want one which is tied to a primary residence. This is a person's home and it is the place where they live.

A home is much more than just a building, especially to a family with children, and there is an emotional attachment to it.

When someone moves into a neighborhood, they begin to make connections. Their children attend the local school. The family might join the local church or become involved with other groups. They begin to put down roots and they will not want to leave, if they can help it.

Part of the reason I love investing in these non-performing junior loans is that it allows me to help people out of a really difficult time in their lives.

There have been plenty of cases where I purchased a note, researched the borrower and found they are a hardworking and honest person. They have a family, they want the best for them and they need help.

Investing in notes works because you are able to contact the borrower, explain the situation, and then show them how they can stay in their home.

These are people who are facing eviction and may not know there are other options out there. When I finally get them on the phone, many are relieved to be talking about an actual *solution*.

The bottom line is that I'm looking for people who are happy in their home and do not want to leave. They are willing to work with us because we offer them a way out from under their mounting financial burdens.

We may not erase the loan completely but we offer a payment plan which is designed to work within their budget. We are effectively saving them from losing their home. The different solutions which we offer our homeowners will be covered soon.

Going Further

At this point, you have learned what a note is, where it comes from, and how to buy one. While all of this may be interesting, it does little to tell us about how a note becomes a profitable investment.

Once you have purchased a note, it is time to contact the borrower and begin working out a solution.

The first step in this process is called "The Wake-Up." This is when we attempt to contact the borrower in a number of ways which we hope will prompt them to contact us.

There are a number of laws and regulations which will have to be followed during this process and we have developed a few unique tricks to make sure you have all your bases covered.

The next chapter will detail the Wake-Up process, offer some insight into how we have done it in the past and then explain some of the most successful techniques we have used.

The information contained in the next few chapters is exciting and will create a road map which you can follow to have success profiting from non-performing notes.

Chapter Six

The Borrower Wake-Up

Now that you're familiar with the process of purchasing notes, it's time to focus on making money. Your profit is made when you buy...but *realized* when you sell.

Every investment is designed to make its investor money, but each one does so in a different way. What makes non-performing notes truly unique is that this profit comes from a direct, one-on-one relationship with the borrower.

This means that, unlike a dispassionate, numbers-only investment like stocks, bonds, and mutual funds, you have more *direct control* over your likelihood of success. The better you are at this part, the higher your Return on Investment can be.

In order to realize your profit, you'll be working directly with the person who originally took out the loan. The first thing we have to do to begin building a relationship is to contact them. This is what we call the "Wake-Up Process".

The *goals* here are to 1) inform them of your intent to pursue the debt, and 2) encourage them to contact you and begin working on a solution.

We have actually developed a very effective process for

"waking up" these borrowers. It was created based on years of experience with countless notes and debtors.

Finding the Borrower

When I purchase a note, I get specific information about the borrower along with it. This will be as up-to-date as possible, but there is no guarantee it will be completely current.

Usually, you'll get a credit report and information that is 6 months old or less—but it is also possible that the borrower has moved or changed contact information since then.

It's important to remember these are delinquent loans. This means the borrower has been ignoring their obligations and this might have gone on for a number of years.

They might also be hiding, so to speak, although if they are still living in the property then at least you know where they are most of the time.

Many of the notes you'll find, in fact, have been delinquent for a few years. During this time, the borrower may not have been contacted much, if at all. They may have received a letter or a phone call, but other than that the previous lenders have basically left them alone.

The first thing I will usually do is to try contacting the borrower using the information I have. Generally, this is just a simple phone call which lets me know if I have the right contact information.

If the person who answers is not my borrower, I might try to send a letter or use any other bit of information I have.

Sometimes these notes will have cosigners; and if so, I will try contacting them as well.

If all of these attempts fail, then I am faced with a situation in which the borrower needs to be tracked down. To do this, I will use a number of resources, including websites which allow me to search a variety of databases.

There have even been a few cases where I had to hire a private investigator to find this person. If you do a Google search for "skip tracer," you'll find several places where you can get someone's current contact information for only $20-25.

Laws and Regulations

There are different laws and regulations to be aware of when contacting the borrower, and laws are different depending on which state in which the property is located In nearly every state, though, the borrower must be informed of any change to their loan.

This means you have to make sure they know their loan has been sold. In addition to this, you need to let them know you are the one who purchased it.

Following this is important because if the borrower can prove that you failed to follow any regulations, they could potentially have the loan thrown out (though it doesn't happen often).

This is true for anything involving notes, and strict adherence to laws and regulations is always a must.

While this may seem like a bit of a hassle, there is actually a good reason for it. Only a few years ago, lenders were handing out loans like it was going out of fashion.

Many of these loans were given to people who simply could not afford the payments—especially when a variable interest rate was added into the equation. This, naturally, led to a lot of defaulted loans and subsequent foreclosures.

There was an immense public outcry during this time. People were blaming banks and other lenders for creating this situation with "predatory lending practices."

Whether or not what these banks did was valid is a discussion for a different book. The fact remains, however, that the government had to do something to calm the angry public.

What they did was begin creating laws pertaining to what can and can't be done when attempting to collect a debt. These new laws created a number of hoops which lenders now have to jump through if they want to get their money back.

As someone who purchases notes, you are legally considered a lender and these laws will apply to you.

California Homeowners Bill of Rights

One of these laws was passed in California is called the California Homeowners Bill of Rights. This law describes a number of things which lenders must do before they can move forward with their attempts to settle a debt.

The purpose is to ensure that borrowers are kept up to date on the status of their debts and are aware of who owns their loan. These types of laws are moving quickly across the country.

This actually protects both the borrower (who is no longer in the dark) and the lender, who could lose their money if the loan was thrown out in court.

While this law is full of a lot of legal language, one of the fundamental requirements states that as a lender, you must contact the borrower *three times, in three different ways, prior to filing any type of foreclosure action.*

You need to let them know what happened to their loan, that you now own it and that you will be attempting to collect the money you are owed. Fortunately, we have developed something which not only covers this type of law but also helps us initiate that first productive discussion with our borrower.

The Shock and Awe Package

The Shock and Awe Package is something I developed over the years and have found to be incredibly effective. Its name comes from President Bush's campaign of the same name in the Middle East, shortly after the September 11th attacks.

The first thing he did before he even sent any troops in was to begin a bombing campaign which was designed to shock the local government. It was sending a message, pure and simple.

President Bush wanted them to know we were both serious about pursuing this conflict and well equipped to do so.

My Shock and Awe Package is designed to do the exact same thing, albeit in a less destructive manner. The purpose is to grab my borrower's attention and let them know I am both serious about pursuing this debt and powerful enough to do so successfully.

The goal is to have them contact me and begin working on a solution.

In addition to this, the package also covers me in terms of laws like CA HOBOR (CA Homeowners Bill of Rights).

Since I am required to contact them anyway, I decided I might as well use this as an opportunity to be productive and get closer to my goal.

I will usually include the same things in each package I send. These are:

A letter of introduction

This is simply a letter which tells them who I am, why I am contacting them, and how they can get in touch with me.

I will often include some information about myself and my company in an effort to show that I am professional and have done this in the past.

If (and when) you can show that you have successfully negotiated arrangements with borrowers in the past, they will be more likely to work with you. So after your first successful workout, make sure to get a testimonial in writing from the borrower.

A copy of the Note

I always include a copy of the note and I would suggest you do the same. While this may only be required in some states, it is helpful in nearly every case.

There have been plenty of times when I called a borrower and they tried to tell me they did not have a loan.

By including a copy of the note with their signature and the date on which it was signed, there is no way for them to argue with me about that.

A copy of the Deed in Trust or Mortgage

I also include the paperwork which shows their home was used as collateral for the loan. The point of this is to let them know that I have the right to initiate foreclosure on their home if I choose to.

A Demand Letter

This is simply a letter in which I formally request payment on their loan. This is a requirement in many states but it is also a practical idea.

The borrower has just received this package of information and they may not know what to do with it. The demand letter will tell them what your intentions are and hopefully convince them to contact you.

Looks Matter

So far, we have only covered the shocking element of the package. The information we include in it is designed to shock the borrower and let them know that someone is very focused on their case.

Most people, however, will generally just ignore any official looking letters. This is especially true for anyone attached to a delinquent loan.

They have likely received quite a few collections letters and have taken to dropping them in the trash without even opening them. If we really want this package to be effective, we need to make sure they will open it.

I had considered this problem for quite some time until one day it dawned on me...This needed to be more than just a collection of letters and photocopies. It needed to be a full package.

I decided I would actually invest a small bit of money in its creation to really drive home the element of awe. This is not a time to be cheap after investing all that you have in purchasing the note.

So I have all of the necessary information printed onto nice paper and compiled into a binder. This binder itself is attractive and official-looking. Then I take all of this and put it together in an actual UPS, USPS or Fed-Ex Box and have it sent out to the borrower.

This final step really is crucial and it is part of what makes this package so successful. What I realized is that people might ignore official-looking letters but they will almost never ignore a package. Don't you open every package you receive?

If they have been expecting a package in the mail, they

will open it. If they haven't been expecting such a package they will be just as likely to open it out of curiosity.

On top of this, sending it as a package gives me the ability to track its delivery. I can literally follow the package on my computer and see if it is delivered or not.

Since the package needs to be signed for, the person delivering it will not simply leave it on the front porch. I can see when they attempted to deliver it and exactly what time it was accepted.

The borrower can never claim that I didn't send it to them because I have all of the proof I need.

This package may cost a few dollars, but it really is an investment in your own success. I had struggled for a while trying to get borrowers to contact me.

Once I started using this package, my success rate improved dramatically. It's a simple trick which plays on human nature but it works incredibly well.

At this point, we will hopefully have made contact with the borrower and convinced them to at least begin discussing the situation. This, however, is not always the case and sometimes a borrower may be hard to reach. If the Shock and Awe Package never gets delivered, or on the rare occasion that it fails to work, there is still something we can do.

Knock Knock!

There have been a few cases where I had failed to get in touch with the borrower, no matter what I did. I knew the person still lived in the house, which was attached to the note but they have been hiding from me.

If the property was only a short drive away, I might consider going there and knocking on the door. Since many of my notes were for properties all over the country, this wasn't possible.

I eventually discovered one of the most useful tools in my collection. I had hired private investigators in the past to help track down borrowers, but what I found was many of them will offer a "Door Knock Service" and this is exactly what it sounds like.

There are private investigators all over the country and you should have no trouble finding one near the location of the house. For a small fee, you can hire one to physically drive out to the address and knock on the borrower's door. What I do is plan to have them call me when they get there and keep me on the line.

The investigator will knock on the door and explain to the borrower who they are. They then tell the borrower that I am currently on the phone and would like to talk to them.

The fact that someone showed up at their house, phone in hand, is often enough to really shock and surprise the borrower.

What to Expect

In a perfect world, we would buy the note, call the borrower, and start receiving payments by the end of the month. Our job, unfortunately, is rarely this easy. If it was, the banks would never have sold the note in the first place.

The reality of the situation is that only about 10% of the borrowers will respond to that first phone call. You have to try several times.

You may, of course, get lucky. Perhaps you purchased a really good note and all it took was a simple phone call to work everything out. Most of the time, however, you will need to try at least one of the methods I've described.

Both the Shock and Awe Package and the door knock

services are extremely effective, but you should also be prepared for what happens when you finally get the borrower on the phone.

Many of these notes, as I've said, have been delinquent for a number of years. This loan is something the borrower has not only ignored but may have entirely forgotten about.

Since the banks were so overwhelmed with delinquent loans, they simply gave up on trying to contact each borrower. Years have passed and the borrower may think the loan has simply gone away.

When they begin receiving packages and phone calls, however, many of them become defiant, defensive, and often a little hostile.

The only reason I mention this is because I want you to be prepared. If you have had to pursue the borrower in one way or another, they are not likely to be happy about talking to you. They thought they were free from this obligation and now they are being forced to face their problems once again.

Many borrowers will try to argue with you and this is why we include such detailed information in our Shock and Awe Package.

One of the most common things a borrower will say to you is that there is no loan. They will try to tell you there is no note in their name and it is not attached to their property.

By including a copy of the note, we can win this argument before it even begins.

Here is a short list of other common objections and how they can be overcome:

The loan has been "Charged off"

This is something a borrower might say to you. Some of

them have still been keeping a close eye on their finances and will have seen a recent credit report.

The report will label their loan, a second mortgage in this case, as being "Charged off". Many borrowers mistakenly believe this means the loan is gone.

The best way to combat this is to explain what a charge off is. When the bank sells the note, they will consider it as charged off and no longer on their ledger. The bank is done with this loan and will not pursue it any longer.

It does not, in any way, mean the loan is gone. It can be a good idea to include this information in the Shock and Awe Package as well.

My loan is with X Bank

Even if they have been ignoring the debt, many borrowers still admit to having taken out a loan. They will tell you the loan was with Wells Fargo, or whatever bank or lender might have issued it.

The implication is they have no obligation to you and you have no right to request payment.

Combating this will involve a little bit of education. It is important to make sure the borrower understands that you have legally purchased the note through an assignment recorded in the county courthouse and they are now obligated to pay you.

Once again, it might be a good idea to include this information in the package.

The junior lien can't foreclose

Foreclosure is a bit of a dirty word these days and fortunately it's not something we will generally need to worry about. It is, however, something we may need to threaten from time to time.

Some people will simply not agree to work with you unless there are some serious repercussions, and foreclosure is the most serious action we can take.

The problem is many of them will not believe the junior lien can foreclose. They may have been operating under this false assumption for some time and have even been paying off their first mortgage.

Again, informing them that you are not only able to foreclose but intend to do so if they refuse to work with you is the best way to win this argument.

I don't have any money

This is a common objection and may be the only one which is true. Some people simply do not have the money they need to cover all of their debts and bills.

This could, in fact, be the reason their second mortgage has defaulted despite their best efforts. In some cases, the person may be more than willing to start repaying the loan if only they could afford to do so.

The best solution to this objection is to be as compassionate and understanding as possible.

You want to impress upon them the idea that you are not like the other debt collectors who have been harassing them.

You are willing to work with them, to go over everything and take the time to develop a solution they can actually follow.

This is, essentially, what we are trying to do with every one of our borrowers. By treating them differently than other debt collectors, you can achieve different results.

Stay Professional

I will be the first one to admit that working with borrowers can be rather frustrating during the first few steps. It's not a lot of fun. In all honesty, you can't blame these people for being evasive or defensive.

These are people who have found themselves in a tough situation, who have been harassed by debt collectors coming at them from all angles. To them, you are just another annoyance and they want you to go away.

Most of the people I end up speaking to are civil and polite, even if they aren't entirely convinced of my desire to help them. There are, however, plenty of people who will get nasty on the phone.

Some people do this because it has worked for them in the past. They will go from zero to horrible in no time flat and it is nothing more than a tactic designed to throw you off. Don't let it stop you!

The most important thing to remember when dealing with borrowers is to always, without fail, be as professional as possible. You must never lose your cool, *Never* let them bring you down to their level.

You must always try to be apologetic, understanding, and sincere in your desire to help. Someone may begin to rant and rave but, if you don't play into it, they will eventually run out of energy and will have to listen.

Dealing with people professionally is also important because it protects you as a lender. There is a huge collection of new laws which describe what could be constituted as harassment.

Basically, you are allowed to take actions to pursue a debt up until to a certain point. You are not allowed to call them excessively, curse at them, or threaten things which are not within your reach.

If you do any of this, you could be taken to court and the loan will be thrown out. On top of that, you may be forced to pay a fine to the borrower. If nothing else, it will turn off the borrower and some of them will dig in their heels and refuse to work with you even when it's in their best interest.

Some of these borrowers will understand this. They know that if they can get you to lose your cool they will have won and the loan will be gone.

No matter how tempting it may be to go off on someone, you must resist the urge and stay professional.

Moving Forward

At this point we have purchased our notes, followed our legal obligations and have gotten in touch with our borrower. This first conversation is really all we are aiming for at this point the entire process.

We call this the "Borrower Wake-Up" because we are essentially waking them up to the reality of their situation.

Now that we have managed to initiate a discussion, we will need to start on the process whereby we understand the borrower's situation, take a look at their resources and develop a plan which works for them. We call this the "Work-Out" phase and it is arguably the most important part of investing in non perming junior liens.

It might seem impossible to come up with a working solution for someone who lacks the money to pay back their loans.

To be completely honest, this part of investing in notes can often be the most labor-intensive. But it's pretty much over once you have an agreement worked out with the borrower making payments to you.

Fortunately, we've been able to come up with a few useful techniques and suggestions which will have you well on your way to solving your borrower's problems. The next chapter will cover the work-out process in detail.

CHAPTER SEVEN:

The Borrower Work-out

At this point, you know what a note is and where it comes from. I have also covered who sells these notes and how you can go about purchasing them.

The previous chapters have outlined some of the basic requirements for a good note and you should be familiar with the way in which I choose the notes I buy.

Once you have a note, you need to contact the borrower so you can begin working on a solution together. This is the "Wake Up" process and it is one of the most important steps when investing in notes.

Simply put, if you can't get the borrower to talk to you then you can never hope to create a solution. This solution is how we make our money and this chapter will cover it in detail.

When you finally have the borrower on the phone, the next step is to attempt a "Work-out" arrangement with them.

Our Goal

Before I go in to the specifics of the borrower work-out process, it'll be helpful to gain a better understanding of your goal.

You have purchased these notes as an investment. As with any investment, you are hoping to make a return which exceeds the price you paid for it.

With notes, this return will come directly from either the borrower or the property. More often than not, the money you make will be paid directly by the borrower.

This is why the "Wake-up" process is so important. Not only do I want them to contact me...I want to be sure the borrower understands the situation.

The borrower needs to know their loan has not gone away and is in fact now in the hands of someone who intends to do something.

Most importantly, however, I also want them to understand I am here to help them.

This is the truth, and it's important that you approach each borrower with this mentality. Your borrower is someone who is struggling through a very hard time in their life.

They will probably have debt collectors calling them, cancellation notices piling up, and they may have recently lost their job. No one else is offering them any sort of mutually-beneficial solution and this is why our process works.

Your goal is not just to make money from this person. What you really want to do is create a solution which benefits *both of you.*

I will work with the borrower to understand their situation and then create something which helps them stay in their home, reduce their debt, and relieve them of this heavy financial burden.

I'm more than just a distanced investor. I am offering them a way out of a situation which may have been quite bleak and hopeless only a few weeks before. Keep in mind that you can offer them the option of paying off the debt at a reduced price.

This is why I always say you need to be as compassionate and understanding as possible. When you begin working with these borrowers, you'll quickly realize they are real people.

Many of them have found themselves in this situation through no fault of their own. You'll empathize with a lot of them and that is the key to a successful work-out.

One of the things I've always found rewarding about this type of investment is the gratitude people often have. Our economy has not been doing well lately at the time of this writing, and many people have simply run out of options.

They may try to talk to debt collectors but the only solution they're given is to pay the full amount of the debt.

Most people don't have that kind of money lying around, so what is their incentive to try? Until now, no one has tried to empathize with them or treat them like a real human being.

Many of these people are very worried about their future. They have purchased a home and intended to start a life. Now all of their plans are in shambles and they have no idea what will happen to them and their family.

When I start working with them and they see that I'm really trying to help them, they are often extremely grateful and happy to talk to me.

So you should always remember you're here to help these people. Your ultimate goal may include making a return on your investment, but that return is earned by helping someone out of a difficult period in their lives.

Your goal is to create a plan which works for both you

and your borrower. This really is the secret to why investing in non-performing junior liens works.

Developing a Clear Picture

Before you begin creating a solution, you'll want to understand your borrower. You need to develop an accurate profile of who they are and what type of person you'll be dealing with. This often doesn't involve financial information in any way.

While it can be tempting to begin talking about money during that first conversation, I always try to resist this urge. You need to remember you are building a long term relationship with this borrower.

Some of these loans may last for a decade or more and you simply must be able to trust each other. Your borrower needs to trust you just as much as you need to be able to rely on them.

The first step in the work-out process is building this trust and rapport. I like to begin our relationship by talking about the borrower on a personal level. I will ask about their life, their kids, their family, and their hobbies.

I am trying to develop a deeper understanding of who this person is so I can begin to consider different solutions.

Here is an example of who your borrower might be:

Joe Borrower is a 36 year old football fan with two high school aged daughters. His wife works part time selling her handmade jewelry but is otherwise unemployed.

Joe had been an electrical engineer but the company moved last year and he lost his job. He managed to get a new job but the pay is much lower. He also has a first mortgage on his home as well as two car payments.

In addition to all of this, he is concerned about paying for college, a problem which is only a few years away.

By talking with the borrower as if they're a real person, you'll be able to understand things from their perspective. You will be able to see their situation through their eyes and you'll know what this person is most concerned with.

Equally as important, however, is the fact that your borrower has never encountered a person like you.

Legally speaking, you have every right to demand payment, foreclose on their home and never think twice about your borrower or their family. What makes them want to work with you is they know you are legitimately concerned for their family's future.

This short period of rapport and trust building will pay off later. Once I've gotten the borrower to wake up and realize they need to deal with this problem, I'll want to convince them to work with me.

I want them to know I am here to help and will do whatever I can to find a solution which works for them. If they trust me, they'll be far more likely to help me find an answer which benefits both of us.

All Cards on the Table

Now that your borrower knows who you are and is willing to work with you, you'll need to assess their financial situation. Since you'll be creating a solution for their financial problems, you need to have an accurate depiction of their resources.

Simply put, you have to find out what you're working with before you can create a plan which fits.

You will probably already have a copy of your borrower's credit report but there are some other important pieces of information you'll need. Here is a short list of items you should request:

❖ **Credit Reports**

If you don't already have one, you need to pull your borrower's credit report. The laws for this can vary from state to state but you will generally need their permission to do so.

Since you have already established a relationship built on trust and mutual understanding, this should be a fairly easy thing to acquire.

❖ **Financial Statements**

Almost everyone will have a bank, savings and retirement account but some people will have more than one. They may have a personal account as well as a joint account which they share with their spouse.

You need to get information relating to every account in their name so you can understand how much available money they have.

❖ **Salary and Employment Information**

Most of your borrowers will be employed. Some of them will have a spouse who is also employed. You should request any information which pertains to how much they get paid, whether it is hourly or a salary.

This is important because it will help you understand how much money is coming in each month, a factor which can greatly affect the ultimate solution.

❖ **Expenses**

Determining how much money is coming in each month is important but so is finding out how much is going out. I always request some information relating to my borrower's bills and expenses.

I do this so I will know how much of their monthly income is already spoken for and how much is left over. Expenses can include things like bills and utilities as well as their budget for food and entertainment.

You should also remember to ask about both home and auto insurance payments.

❖ **Other Debts**

If your borrower is behind on their loan it can be a safe bet that they will be behind on other debts as well. Since you are purchasing second mortgages, almost all of your borrowers will still have a first mortgage which is not paid off.

Many people will also have credit card debts, student loan debts and possibly even a third mortgage. Most people who live in a house will also have at least one car which they are likely still paying for.

All of these debts will affect the amount of resources they have.

❖ **Other Resources**

Some people will have other financial resources which they may not consider when speaking with you.

Plenty of people have retirement accounts such as a 401(k) or an IRA. Some borrowers may even own stocks or have invested in other ways.

These are all resources which can be used to help solve their current problem and it is important to request this information whenever it's applicable.

❖ **Future Resources**

Future resources are essentially anything which will improve the borrower's financial situation in the near future.

This can include things such as settlement payments from a court case or even an inheritance which is still in escrow. Some borrowers may not be working because of an injury and they're still waiting on the settlement payments from this case.

This is important because these future resources will change the whole picture in a short period of time.

The purpose of all this is to simply understand what you're working with. Your plan needs to fit into your borrower's budget so you need to know what that budget is. All of this information is important and the more you can find, the more helpful the work-out solution will be.

The Plan

In the majority of all cases, the solution will come in the form of a monthly payment plan. This plan takes into consideration both the amount of money owed on the loan and the resources available to the borrower.

These loans are created with their own payment plans, but these payments are currently beyond your borrower's financial abilities.

Your plan will be different. You'll assess their finances, look at the loan and then come up with a plan you feel your borrower can easily follow.

The goal here is not to create a plan which eats up the last bit of their money every month. You want them to be able to comfortably pay it month after month—and at the same time be happy to do so.

This is why it's so important to understand your borrower's monthly expenses. If they get to the point where they need to decide between buying food for their family and sending you the monthly payment, they will almost always choose to miss that payment.

An effective plan is one which they can follow while still living their normal lives. Don't try too hard to arrange an unrealistic payment amount.

Arrears

The first thing to consider when creating a work-out plan is called the arrears. This is the debt which has accrued while the borrower was not making payments.

This includes the monthly payments they have missed as well as any late fees or penalties which may have been added on. While it is possible to wave these arrears payments, I never suggest it.

The arrears are important because this is the first payment you'll receive. This person's loan is delinquent and it needs to be made current. In order to do this, however, they need to begin paying off the money they already owe.

Since this loan has not been performing for a number of years, the arrears can be quite significant.

The amount of money owed in arrears could, in fact, be almost enough to cover your investment cost. Let's say, for example, you purchased a non-performing junior lien for $5,000.

This loan has gone unpaid for a few years and the arrears have now grown to about $4,000.

When the borrower pays off the arrears you will have already made back most of your investment cost. $1,000 of monthly payments later and every dollar you receive will be profit!

I will generally try to get the arrears paid off in one lump sum. This is mostly because getting the payment all at once is simply easier and I am handling quite a few different notes.

You do, however, have to be realistic and if the person can't afford to pay it off in one lump sum then you should allow them to pay it in increments. Just makes sure the arrears are covered as quickly as possible.

Monthly Payments

Once the arrears have been covered, the loan is now current. This is great for your borrower because it immediately improves their credit rating and they no longer have to worry about foreclosure. It is also great for you because you are already starting to make your money back.

The next step is to develop a continuing payment plan which your borrower can follow every month.

As I've said, you want the monthly payments to fit into your borrower's budget. To achieve this, you will usually need to reduce the amount of money they have to pay each month.

This person may have taken out a loan at a time when they could afford $1,000 a month. Something happened, however, and this is simply beyond their budget right now.

Don't try too hard to collect the large regular monthly payment, as something is always better than nothing in your position.

Since you are now the owner of the loan and legally speaking, have become the lender, you can modify the loan in a number of ways. Most mortgages will have a time limit and this can be 10, 20, or even 30 years.

The monthly payments are based on this limit. If the loan is for $50,000, for example, and the monthly payment is $1,000, it will take 50 months to pay off the loan. This does not consider the interest, though.

The solution I've found to be most effective in the majority of cases is to extend the loan to a point at which the payments will fit into my borrower's budget.

Turning a 10-year loan into a 20-year loan, for example, could potentially cut the monthly payments in half. Someone may not be able to afford $1,000 a month but

$500 a month is well within their resources.

What I'll do is develop a payment plan and then sit down and explain it to my borrower. I'll tell them how it fits into their budget, what the changes are, and how it will work for both of us. Sometimes they will say it is still beyond their reach and I will need to tweak it.

Why This Works

This type of solution works for a number of reasons. As an investor, you have just potentially recovered the majority of your investment cost by receiving a payment for the arrears.

You have helped this person get their loan current and they are now willing to work with you on a long term payment plan.

Extending the length of the loan works because of the interest payments. There is interest attached to almost every loan and this is how lenders make their money.

When you turn a 10-year loan into a 20-year loan, you are effectively doubling the amount of interest payments you will receive. By changing the loan to make it more affordable for your borrower, you are actually increasing your overall profits.

This payment plan also works for the borrower because they are now able to make payments on their mortgage and continue living in their home.

You can also begin reporting their on-time payment history and help them improve their credit, which benefits both of you.

This is an incredible relief for a lot of people because most lenders and debt collectors simply won't do this. Most of these institutions don't care and will not attempt to create a plan which actually works for the borrower.

Other Options

Payment plans have accounted for about 60-70% of all my notes. This is the way the majority of your notes will be made to start performing again. This solution works best for cases with strong emotional equity.

What I mean is you need to have a borrower who wants to *stay in their house.*

Short Sale

Sometimes, however, you will run into a borrower who isn't interested in staying at that location. Perhaps they've been wanting to move, maybe they recently got divorced, or their children have moved out and they want to downsize.

No matter what the reason may be, it can be hard to convince someone to follow a payment plan when they don't care about losing the house.

This is when I will usually offer a solution in the form of a short sale. A short sale is a method of paying off a debt which is tied to a property or other solid asset.

It is called a short sale because it will not cover the entirety of the debt but it will cover some or most of it.

When a short sale happens, the money earned from the sale goes to the lender to help pay off the debt. There will usually be some debt left over and this is called the deficiency.

In some states, the borrower is still responsible for paying down this deficiency. In states like California, however, the deficiency is waived once the short sale has happened.

This can be a great solution for the right borrower. This person may want to leave their house but they have been stuck under their mortgages. They can't afford to pay them off immediately and there are still many years left on the loan.

By offering them a short sale, I am giving them a way out from under this house. I am effectively granting their wish to be able to move.

A short sale works for me because the money earned from selling the house will generally exceed the amount I paid for the note. Let's say I purchased a note for $10,000 but the value of the loan is $100,000 and the value of the property is about $90,000.

The house is put up for sale and sold for $75,000 which is then sent to me to cover the mortgage.

In this example, I have spent $10,000 on a note and made $65,000 in profit in a very short period of time. I honestly don't even need to worry about the arrears or the interest payments because the profit is high.

Foreclosure

Foreclosure is something I will cover in detail in the coming chapters. I've included it here simply because it is technically a solution to your borrower's debt.

Foreclosure is essentially the act of taking possession of the collateral used for a debt which has gone unpaid. This is something which has been used by the banks to recover some of the money they lost on bad loans.

Since we are investing in notes and not real estate, however, you'll want to avoid foreclosure whenever possible. When you foreclose on a borrower's home you will become the owner of the property.

While a note may be a somewhat passive investment, owning a foreclosed house usually requires a lot more work (and liability).

The money to cover the remaining debt is earned either

by selling the house or renting it out. Both options come with a number of different problems and none of them really fit into our investment strategy.

In addition to this, foreclosure can be a long, expensive procedure and there are new laws being created every year which make it even more difficult.

You are also legally allowed to foreclose on a property once you have filed a notice of default and sale. At this point, you could decide to simply foreclose on the property and try to sell it or rent it out.

Keep in mind that this is not what investing in notes is all about. When you foreclose, you are turning a note investment into a real estate investment.

Refinancing

Refinancing a loan is another option, but it has recently fallen out of favor due to tight lending practices.

When a borrower chooses to refinance a loan, they'll have to work with a company that offers this service. They will generally take out a new loan and use that money to pay off the original loan.

The interest rate will often be rather high and the penalties can be excessive. Most importantly, the borrower will now be working with someone else who will not be as concerned for their well-being.

This can create a situation in which the borrower has gone from one bad spot to another and they have not really solved any of their problems.

Despite all of this, refinancing a loan is one option you might have available if they can qualify. When the borrower takes out the new loan, they will be able to pay off your loan in full.

This means you will get the full amount still owed,

which includes interest and possible late fees, in one lump sum.

The Typical Work-out

Every note will be different and you may need to get creative when solving a few problems. The majority of the notes you purchase, however, will generally follow the same formula.

Since I have presented a lot of information in this chapter, I feel it would be a good idea to give you a quick rundown of a typical work-out scenario.

Step #1: You find and purchase the note.

This was the subject of the second chapter. You have done your research, found the notes you want and purchased them.

Step #2: You contact the borrower.

This is the "Wake-up" process described in the previous chapter.

Step #3: You assess their situation.

This the period of time you spend understanding your borrower's current financial situation. You'll develop a certain level of trust and rapport and then begin looking at their resources.
This is also the step that requires the most participation from the borrower because you need accurate information.

Step #4: You formulate a plan.

Using the information you received in the previous step, you will begin creating a work-out plan which your borrower can follow. This plan should be as detailed as possible before it's presented to the borrower.

A typical plan might look something like this:

> ➤ $4,500 payment for the arrears to bring the loan current
> ➤ An extension of the loan from 10 to 20 years
> ➤ A new interest rate which may be lower than the last one
> ➤ $500 monthly payment for the life of the loan
> ➤ Set penalties for late or missed payments

Step #5: You present it to the borrower.

Once you have come up with a plan which you feel will work for both of you, you'll present it to the borrower. At this point, you need to make sure they understand everything about it.

You should focus on how this plan is beneficial to them and how it will improve their situation.

The borrower will then either approve the plan or explain why it doesn't work. If it won't work, then you'll repeat steps 4 and 5 until they agree to something.

Step #6: You draw up a loan agreement.

This agreement will basically explain the changes made to the loan and what is expected from both the lender and the borrower. It will also list the different payments as well as the penalties for nonpayment.

Once it is drawn up, you have the borrower sign it.

Step #7: You collect the arrears

As I've said, you should always address the arrearage. This payment is an important part of your investment strategy and it needs to be received first. It's okay if it needs to be broken up into smaller increments, but you must be sure you are getting this payment if possible.

Step #8: You collect the monthly payments

This is the passive part of your investment and it is how you will make the majority of your money. At this point, there is very little for you to do other than cash this check every month.

In a short period of time, all of this money will be profit because your investment costs have been covered.

Step #9: You deal with problems

These loans can last for a number of years and there are a variety of problems which can pop up. Most of these are easily fixed and this is where that relationship with the borrower comes into play.

This portion of the process is generally handled by a servicer and this will be explained in the coming chapters.

Step #10: You exit!

There are a number of different ways to complete the loan. Some people will simply keep paying until it is finished. A lot of borrowers though, will move, refinance, sell the house and potentially pay off your loan in full.

In addition to this, you can sell this note to someone else as a re-performing note for much more than you paid for it. Different exit strategies will be covered later.

This is how the majority of your non-performing note investments can work. There will be some slight differences and you may begin to develop your own tactics.

Overall, this is a fairly straightforward process and one which actually helps the borrower get their life back together. This is what I mean by a win/win situation. You are making money while helping people at the same time.

This work-out process will account for about 60-70% of all the notes you will work through. There are about 20% of borrowers who will make this process difficult but will ultimately agree to some sort of a solution.

Moving Forward

By now you should have all of the basic information you need to understand how investing in non performing notes works.

You know where to find them, how to choose the best, how to contact the borrower, and a few of the ways in which you'll be making your money.

The next chapter will cover one of a note investor's greatest fears. Since we are dealing with people who may be stuck under a significant amount of debt, bankruptcy is always a possibility. M

any people, in fact, will file for bankruptcy based on poor and inaccurate information.

Fortunately for us, bankruptcy is hardly something to be worried about and the next chapter will explain why.

CHAPTER EIGHT:

Bankruptcy and the Junior Lien

Now that you have a good understanding of how this industry works, I want to cover some of the biggest challenges you may run into.

After you've purchased and handled a few different notes, you'll begin to realize that each case is different.

This investment really is all about the borrowers and you need them to agree to work with you. Eventually, however, you may run into a borrower who thinks they can get around this debt.

The most common way they try to do this is through bankruptcy—and it is one of the greatest fears many beginner non performing note investors have.

I actually had the same fear when I first started. I thought I would lose everything if a borrower decided to file bankruptcy. This fear, as I soon found out, was completely unfounded.

I used to avoid any notes tied to a borrower who had filed bankruptcy but now I will seek them out. Over the course of the next few pages you'll find out why.

Why Bankruptcy?

The textbook reason why people file bankruptcy is because they are drowning in debt. They owe more money than they can ever hope to pay back and the bankruptcy should help them solve this problem.

While this may be what bankruptcy was intended for, most people choose to file for it because of bad information.

You can actually find evidence of this bad information by simply driving down the highway or watching television. There are countless ads offering bankruptcy services and they claim this is the solution to every one of your problems.

Just give them a call, they say, and all of your debt will be gone. On top of this, many family members will try to suggest the same thing.

This is an intriguing prospect, especially to someone who is having serious financial problems. The idea that all they need to do is make a few phone calls and all of their problems will be solved is one which is hard to resist.

The problem, as these people quickly find out, is that bankruptcy is quite complicated and is far from a cure for all their financial worries.

In practice, most people file bankruptcy because they think it's a good way to avoid paying back their debts. Some people, in fact, will even go so far as to build up a lot of debt and then file for bankruptcy because they think they're getting one over on their creditors.

As an investor in non-performing notes, it is only a matter of time before you run into a borrower who starts talking about bankruptcy.

This can be a worrying prospect to a new investor and I completely understand the fear. Our strategy really focuses on finding a mutually-beneficial solution which the borrower will agree to follow.

The concept of bankruptcy throws a wrench into our process and can sometimes trip people up. Before I start to explain why bankruptcy is not something to fear, you should become familiar with the most common types.

Different Types of Bankruptcy

There are actually a number of different types of bankruptcy but we will only really be concerned with two of them. These are the two most common forms and they will apply to individual debtors.

There are a few forms of bankruptcy which apply to businesses but, since we don't invest in these notes, we don't need to worry about them.

The difference between these two varieties really has to do with the amount of resources a borrower might have. It is usually the court which decides what type of bankruptcy someone will apply for and they base it on things like income, assets which can be liquidated, the amount of money owed, and whether the debt is secured or not.

Secured vs. unsecured debt is a simple concept. Secured debt is what you're dealing with because you have a loan which is tied to real, physical collateral. In this case the collateral is the house.

Unsecured debt, on the other hand, is debt which is not tied to collateral. The most common debt of this type is credit card debt which can be racked up without much more than a signature and a swipe of the card.

Chapter 7

Chapter 7 bankruptcy is called a liquidation and this describes it fairly well. When someone files for Chapter 7 they will have a trustee appointed to them.

This person will look at their resources and compare it to their debts. The trustee will then be put in charge of liquidating assets and distributing the proceeds to the creditors.

What this means is the person filing for this type of bankruptcy is basically throwing in the towel. They are giving up and admitting there is no way they can produce an income so that they can pay off all of this debt.

In this case they will be forced to sell off any nonexempt assets or property and this can include things such as investments, vacation properties or non-essential vehicles.

Chapter 7 bankruptcy would be something to worry about if you were a credit card company. Since this debt is unsecured, it can often be wiped out by a Chapter 7.

Some of the debt may be paid off but, once the bankruptcy is finished, the remainder of the debt can be thrown out.

You, however, own a secured junior lien and don't really need to worry about the debt being wiped out. More importantly, having a borrower get rid of things like credit card payments will actually *free up more resources which they can then use to repay your loan!*

Chapter 13

Chapter 13 bankruptcy is the most common type you will be dealing with. This is called a restructuring because it focuses mainly on helping the person pay off their secured debt. Your note, is a secured junior lien on their home.

When someone qualifies for this type of bankruptcy they'll have a trustee assigned to them. This person will analyze all of the resources and debts and then develop a payment plan.

The person filing for bankruptcy will then be legally obligated to follow this plan for a certain minimum amount of time. This is usually between 36 and 60 months.

If your borrower manages to follow this plan through to completion, some of the remaining debt can be either reduced or removed completely.

When they file for this type of bankruptcy, your borrower is basically admitting they are in over their head. They want to pay off their debt but they can't do it right now, they need some time and some help.

As many people quickly find out, Chapter 13 bankruptcy is not the "get out of jail free" card they had been hoping for.

What Happens

Since you'll be dealing mostly with Chapter 13 bankruptcy, I want to focus on what you should expect when this happens. There will be some cases where you might buy a note and find out the person is already in the middle of bankruptcy proceedings.

Most of the time, however, you will find out about their intention to file during the wake-up process.

Generally, you will contact the borrower, get in touch with them, and begin talking about solutions. This person has been playing with the idea of declaring bankruptcy for a while now and this seems like the perfect time to finally do it.

They might even use it as a threat to get you to leave them alone. The problem, for them, is they don't actually understand the realities of the bankruptcy process.

They File

The first step in any bankruptcy case is the borrower will have to file for it. The court will analyze their situation and then determine which type of bankruptcy they can apply for.

Most of this is done through a lawyer and these lawyers are the ones who keep advertising this process as a solution.

I always suggest that note investors hire their own bankruptcy attorneys. This is a legal case and it needs to be handled correctly to the letter of the law. Since there may be some work involved on your end, hiring a lawyer will make the process that much easier.

On top of this, your attorney will hopefully keep you from making any costly mistakes.

Leave Them Alone

The real purpose of bankruptcy is to give someone time to pay off their debts. Since they may have a lot of debt collectors contacting them, a Chapter 13 bankruptcy will give them a bit of a respite.

When your borrower files for bankruptcy, you are no longer allowed to contact them. The only person you can have contact with is your own lawyer and the borrower's trustee.

When I first ran into this issue I was afraid I would be in the dark. I eventually discovered a great tool which allows me to stay on top of the process without ever talking to the borrower.

When someone files for bankruptcy, they do so through bankruptcy court. The papers they need to file become a matter of public record and you can actually get a hold of this information very easily.

There is a website called PACER.org, which is an acronym for Public Access to Court Electronic Records. It is basically a database which stores all of the records relating to any case filed through the court system. There are records for every court including criminal, family, housing, and, of course, bankruptcy.

This website is free to join, although you may have to pay a small processing fee for downloading the records. Everything about your borrower's bankruptcy case will be available in the PACER databases.

Using PACER, you will be able to follow the case every step of the way and be as up to date on its current status as the borrowers and the attorneys themselves.

In addition to this, you will be able to find out quite a lot of information about the borrower. If they have filed for Chapter 13, as opposed to working with you, it is safe to say they have been a little evasive.

They have likely hidden as much information from you as possible. Going through the Pacer records, however, you can discover things such as hidden assets.

I actually had a note which is a great example of this. The person was evasive and refused to work with me. They eventually filed for Chapter 13 and so I followed the case through PACER.

I discovered this person was receiving a monthly pension which came to over $3,000 a month.

When the case fell through, they tried to tell me they didn't have the money to pay their debt. Since I knew about their pension, I told them I could prove they can afford a $500 monthly payment and they eventually agreed to my Work-Out plan.

Most People Fail

All of this may sound a bit complicated until you become more familiar with the specifics of bankruptcy. The point I'm trying to emphasize is that you should not be afraid of it. I will explain this further in a bit but I wanted to mention the biggest reason why bankruptcy is not something to fear.

Chapter 13 bankruptcy is the most common form you will deal with. As you've read, Chapter 13 requires the debtor to follow the court appointed payment plan for 36 to 60 months.

This really is a long time, especially for someone who is not currently paying off any of their debts. Since most people enter into bankruptcy with the assumption that all of their debt will be gone, many are not happy to find out about this.

To put it simply, this person was looking for a quick and simple solution to their problems with debt. They didn't want to be forced into paying anything and they really didn't want to worry about it for the next 3 to 5 years.

If, for whatever reason, they stop following the plan then the entire case is thrown out and everything goes back to the beginning.

This may be pretty surprising but the statistics for failure in Chapter 13 is about 90%. This is something those billboards and TV ads won't tell you. Only about 10% of people who file for bankruptcy will ever successfully complete it.

The rest are eventually right back where they started. This is why I never worry about it. Out of 100 bankruptcy cases that I might deal with, only about 10 will actually go through.

If you find yourself in this situation the best advice I can give you is to simply be patient. Just leave the note alone, follow the case through PACER, and wait.

There is nothing to worry about and almost nothing for you to do. If your borrower is like 90% of the population, their case will eventually fail and you can go back to trying to work with them.

Why I Like Bankruptcy

When I first started investing in notes I avoided bankruptcy like the plague. I would screen the borrowers before I purchased a note. If the person was either currently in bankruptcy or had filed for it in the past, I would pass on that note.

I was afraid I would lose all of my money because the debt would be wiped out. This fear came from own ignorance about the process.

After I gained some experience, I found out that bankruptcy can actually be a great thing from an investor's standpoint and there are a number of reasons for this.

They're paying me

When I first purchase a note, I'm dealing with a borrower who doesn't want to pay me. Even though about 10% of people will immediately agree to a work-out solution, most borrowers will not want to send me any money.

The wake-up and work-out process takes a bit of time and effort and it can sometimes be frustrating.

When someone files for Chapter 13, however, they are now forced to follow a court appointed payment plan. Since my note is for a secured junior lien, I am going to be part of the payment plan.

The borrower may not have wanted to pay me but now they have no choice. I am now receiving monthly payments from the borrower's trustee.

They're Paying Me More

More importantly, the monthly payments I receive from the trustee is often higher than the payments I would have offered my borrower.

I'm always willing to bend over backwards to develop a work-out solution which this person can follow. I will reduce the payments, extend the loan, waive a part of the arrears, anything I have to do to make this solution work.

The courts, on the other hand, don't really care. They will decide what the person can afford on their own. The borrower can only accept this payment plan or let the case fall apart.

Part of the reason I like bankruptcy is that it makes my life that much easier. Rather than trying to work with the borrower, I now have a trustee taking care of everything and sending me regular monthly payments which are often higher than I would have offered.

Other Debts are Gone

In the previous chapter, I explained how other debts such as credit card debts will eat up a portion of your borrower's resources. Simply put, the more debt your borrower has, the less money they will have to pay you.

Part of the reason I like bankruptcy is it will often remove most, if not all, of this extra debt.

This is especially true for Chapter 7 but holds true for both varieties. When the court looks at your borrower's debt they will break it up into two different categories. They will separate the secured debt from the unsecured debt.

The secured debt will be paid off and the unsecured debt will be thrown out. This is generally credit card debt but it can also be unsecured liens which are junior to your note.

Once this has happened, your borrower no longer needs to worry about this unsecured debt, which usually accounts for the majority of their current financial problems.

The truth is most people will only have a couple of secured debts, mainly their first and second mortgage, so they are now in a much better position to begin paying you the money they owe.

Bankruptcy is Off the Table

The biggest threat with bankruptcy is that it'll keep your borrower from agreeing to the work-out plan. They are under the false assumption that bankruptcy will solve all of their problems without costing them a dime.

This idea is always in the back of their minds and it will keep them from fully committing to your offers for help.

I'm a compassionate person and I always try to educate my borrowers. I tell them bankruptcy is not what they think it is, it's not a simple solution and it will probably not remove their obligations to me as a lender.

A lot of these people, however, think I'm only telling them this because I'm afraid they might go through with it. I never argue...just let them do it if they insist.

You and I both know 90% of all bankruptcy cases will fall apart. This is why I suggest that you just let them do it. It may take a few months, maybe even a year, but that case is going to fall through.

When it does, the borrower has experienced the reality of bankruptcy for themselves. They can no longer retreat to this fantasy of a simple, fast solution.

At this point, they're faced with the reality that you've always been offering help. You have been willing to do whatever it takes to find a solution which works for them. Now that they've been run through the court system, your offers seem a lot more enticing.

Once people have filed for bankruptcy and failed, they are much more likely to work with you. Just try to resist the urge to tell them "I told you so."☺

The Big Picture

Before you started reading this chapter, you were probably a lot like me. Bankruptcy was one of the biggest fears I had.

People would tell me investing in notes was a bad idea because they thought I would be wiped out when my borrower filed for bankruptcy. As with most fears, this was based almost entirely on ignorance.

Now that you understand bankruptcy, what it is, and how it works, you should be able to see how it isn't something to fear. More importantly, bankruptcy can actually be incredibly helpful when dealing with certain borrowers.

A lot of them think they can avoid paying off your note but they soon find this isn't the case. In fact, the opposite of this is usually what happens.

Not only will bankruptcy help you start receiving payments through a trustee but it will put you in an even better position.

When your borrower can manage to get the rest of their debts removed, they now have far more resources to take care of the remaining debts.

While you may have been dealing with someone who

was being pulled in countless directions, you now have a borrower who only needs to focus on their mortgages in an effort to save their home.

Moving Forward

Now that you've discovered how bankruptcy can actually be your friend, I want to move onto the next biggest fear many note investors have.

Part of the reason we have chosen notes is they are not a real estate investment. Investing in real estate can be expensive, complicated, and fraught with a number of common problems.

Foreclosure is something we try to avoid as non performing junior lien investors. The truth is...you will rarely ever have to foreclose on the property attached to your notes.

It is, however, something you need to learn a little about. While it may be rare to actually take possession of a property, threatening foreclosure can be quite useful when it comes to convincing borrowers to work with you.

Foreclosure can be a long process and there is a lot to consider when you initiate it. Understanding a bit about how it works and what you need to do is an important part of becoming a successful non performing note investor.

The next chapter will cover foreclosure in detail and focus on how it applies to you.

CHAPTER NINE:

Foreclosure and the Junior Lien

In the last chapter, I talked about one of the greatest fears which plague new investors. Bankruptcy is something a lot of people worry about but you've learned why it's not so bad and how it can actually help you.

In this chapter, I want to cover the *second-biggest* fear.

Notes are distinctly different from an investment in real estate. We aren't buying physical properties and we're able to avoid the cost and hassle associated with owning an actual house.

These notes are, however, tied to people's homes. As the mortgage holder, you have the legal right to foreclose on this person's home if they refuse to pay you.

The purpose of foreclosure is to recover some of the money lost when a borrower stops paying. It has gained a bit of a bad reputation in the past few years because of the abundance of foreclosures all over the country. Fortunately for us, we are not really interested in following through with a foreclosure.

We don't want to own the property, we just want the monthly payments or a settlement. No matter how long your career in non performing notes might last, you will rarely ever end up taking possession of a home.

You could, theoretically, manage to avoid it altogether and never run into an instance where you will need to go through with it. Despite this fact, initiating foreclosure can be a powerful tool and you need to understand how it works.

Why Foreclose?

In general, banks and other lenders will foreclose on a property in an effort to make back some of the money they've lost on a loan. When the loan is issued, the house is set up as the collateral. Collateral, in any loan, is simply a bit of insurance. It's meant to keep the borrower from skipping out on their obligations. If they do, they will lose the collateral.

Most lenders don't actually want to foreclose. Banks have enough money that if they wanted to start purchasing properties they could do so right away.

In fact, most lenders will try to avoid foreclosure whenever possible and might wait a number of years before even beginning the process. Having a loan fail can affect a lender's reputation and the act of foreclosure is especially unpopular these days.

As a junior lien note holder, you don't want to foreclose either. Your goal, as I've mentioned, is to help this person stay in their home and settle their outstanding debt.

Even though taking possession of the house is not part of our strategy, initiating foreclosure can be useful. The reason for this is the fact that many borrowers will refuse to accept the reality of their situation.

No matter how well you usually handle the wake-up process, some borrowers will not get the picture. For whatever reason, nothing you've done has driven the message home. This is where foreclosure can be a useful tool.

There is a process associated with doing this and each step of it can help shock your borrower into finally working with you.

Myths

There are a few prevalent myths associated with foreclosure from the junior lien position. I've personally run into these misconceptions a number of times and I honestly cannot figure out where they originate from.

You'll often run into someone who simply believes you can't foreclose from the position of the junior lien. Sometimes they received this bad information from a relative and, surprisingly, sometimes they get it from their own lawyer or banker.

In a case like this, it can be hard to convince the borrower to work with you because they think there's nothing you can do. They may worry about their first mortgage because they know it can foreclose but they will think you're just making empty threats.

Initiating foreclosure, however, can be quite a shock to these people and they often scramble to keep their house. Hopefully, you will be able to come to an agreement before you actually take possession.

The truth is that both the first and second mortgage are exactly the same when it comes to foreclosure. The language used in the contract is almost identical, and the provisions are the same.

Simply put, you are just as able to foreclose on the junior lien as you are from the senior lien. If you find yourself speaking with a borrower's lawyer, it might be a good idea to send them a copy of the note with the relevant portion highlighted.

Deed of Trust vs. Mortgage States

If you've found yourself in a situation where you'll need to initiate foreclosure, the first thing you have to determine is whether you're operating in a mortgage state or a deed of trust state.

When someone takes out a loan with the intention of buying a house, they will have to sign a contract. This contract states that the house is the collateral on the loan.

Taking possession of this collateral is handled in one of two ways. Currently, the country is split to the point at which almost half of the states will be deed of trust states and half will be mortgage states.

The main difference between the two is the amount of time and effort needed to complete the foreclosure process.

In a mortgage state, the lender will need take the borrower to court. The court will then review all of the documents and determine if the lender can foreclose.

In a deed of trust state, however, the right to take possession of the collateral is not in question. Foreclosing in a mortgage state can take a long time.

In some states, such as New York, the courts are so backed up there is a 2 to 3 year waiting period before the courts will even look at the case!

In a deed of trust state, on the other hand, the foreclosure process is much faster. Each state will have a different period of time assigned to this process and it can vary quite significantly.

In some states it may take a few months while in others, such as Texas, it can be as fast as 45 days. This is an important consideration and will determine how much time you have to come up with a solution before the final foreclosure sale.

120

How it Works

Foreclosing on a borrower's home will generally follow the same process. This is a multi-step process and each piece of it needs to be handled correctly.

This is a legal matter and failing to follow the relevant regulations can cause you to lose both the case and the money you've invested in the note. Here is a brief overview of the typical foreclosure process:

Step #1: A Notice of Default is filed

The first step in the process is to file a notice of default. This is a legal document which states that the borrower has not held up their end of the loan agreement.

It needs to be filed through the court in the state in which the property is located. There may be some fees associated with this step and I always say you should hire a lawyer or experienced trustee to help you handle it.

Each state, however, will have different requirements which you need to follow before you can file this notice. The basic concept is to make sure the borrower has been contacted and attempts have been made to work with them.

This is part of the reason the wake-up process is so vital. By sending your borrower a demand letter and continuing to try to come up with a solution, you will be able to prove the borrower has simply refused to pay back the money they owe.

What I've found, in my experience, is that this notice of default can often be what was needed to finally get the borrower to wake up. They don't believe I will foreclose, some don't think I'm able to but when they get that notice of default they know I'm serious.

Once they see that I'm about to foreclose on their home,

they will often contact me and try to work out a solution.

Step #2: A Notice of Sale is filed

The next step is to file a notice of sale 90 days later. A typical foreclosure will have the lender taking possession of the property and then putting it up for sale.

The property will often be sold for less than the fair market value because the lender simply wants to make back the money they're owed. A foreclosed property can usually be purchased by anyone and it will be sold through a public auction process.

The notice of sale needs to be published in a newspaper. This newspaper needs to be local to where the property is located. In some cases there will be a number of different newspapers to choose from.

In other cases, however, there may only be one. This will determine the cost to publish the notice.

Newspapers make a good portion of their revenue by charging for this service. Lawyers and business people will need to publish official notices on a regular basis. In areas that are home to multiple newspapers, there is some competition and this tends to keep the prices low.

Sometimes you won't have a choice and the cost will be somewhat outrageous. You have to file this notice of sale so you will just have to pay the cost.

The notice of sale simply says that a certain property is going up for sale. It will describe the property, mention it's a foreclosure sale, and then post the time and location of the auction.

Most foreclosure sales are done on some sort of government property and it might even be held on the steps of the town court house.

If the notice of default was a shock to our borrower

then this notice of sale is a bucket of ice water dumped over their head. ***"Your home will sold to the highest bidder at 10 am on Monday morning on the court house steps"*** is a true wake up call to borrowers in denial.

I've dealt with many borrowers who were refusing to work with me until they saw their house in the newspaper. This can be the final step which is needed to get them to see how serious I am.

Step #3: The house is sold

At this point, the house goes to auction and a number of bidders will show up. Some of these will be investors who have made a career out of purchasing foreclosed properties.

The house is now up for grabs and the highest bidder will become the owner. The proceeds of this sale will then go to the lender in an effort to recover their lost money.

The eviction process generally needs to be handled by the local sheriff and it can sometimes be a rather unpleasant process.

Keep in mind, however, that you gave this person every opportunity to work with you. They were the one who took out the loan and they have refused to make their debts a priority.

The Impact of Foreclosure

Foreclosure is a tool. Banks and lenders will use it to recover lost money while we will use it to give our borrowers that final push. If you ever run into a borrower who is outright refusing to work with you, it's important to remember that they may be dealing with incorrect information.

There have been so many problems with housing loans

over the past few years that most people are fundamentally confused by the whole process.

Most people are not financial experts. Some of your borrowers may be investors, lawyers or accountants but the majority of them will be somewhat ignorant of financial and legal matters.

All they know is people are coming after them for debts they aren't repaying. When you enter the picture, you appear to be essentially just another debt collector who is making empty and hollow threats.

This can make your job that much harder. The first obstacle you have to overcome is convincing the borrower that you are both serious and powerful enough to follow through with your threats.

You can send them letters, knock on their door, and talk to them on the phone but sometimes none of this works. The only way you're going to convince this person to start paying back their loan is to take action.

Foreclosure is the most serious action we can take. We can threaten to foreclose until we're out of breath but nothing will ever have the impact of actually starting it and going through with it.

We are, in fact, preparing to initiate foreclosure from the very beginning.

The Shock and Awe Package, as well as the wake-up process in general, is designed to cover all of the legal prerequisites we need to worry about before foreclosing.

Take Your Time

Using foreclosure as the final wake-up call works because of the nature of the process. Foreclosing on any property is a multi-step process which can often take some time to complete. In some states, as I've mentioned, it can take up to a few years.

Each step in the process can be what finally convinces our borrower to accept the reality of their current situation.

To begin with, in many cases we're dealing with someone who simply doesn't believe we can or will foreclose. Filing the Notice of Default proves that we are not only able to foreclose but have already begun the process.

Some borrowers are shocked because their own lawyer told them this wasn't possible. At this point, they will likely contact you and will be eager to do work something out.

Some borrowers will be more stubborn than this. They may now be convinced that you have the ability to foreclose but they still think you won't do it.

This type of borrower likely knows you don't actually want to take possession of the property. They are going to try to call your bluff and think you will back out if they stay strong.

Once these people have found you've filed a Notice of Sale, however, they realize how mistaken they were. They thought they could hold out until you give up.

What they don't understand is that you're perfectly willing to foreclose if you have to. You've invested money and you will not simply let it disappear. At this point, you should be able to start working with the borrower.

Actually going through with a foreclosure is rare in our business. This investment is about notes and the monthly payments or settlements we can receive from them.

The notes we buy have been filtered to remove any with a high risk of foreclosure. If you're careful with the way you choose your notes, you can avoid ever needing to go through with a foreclosure at all.

I've said it before but I want to emphasize it again—the process of foreclosure is a wonderful tool. Since it takes so much time, we have a bit of a buffer between initiating it and finishing it. This buffer is a great time to continue offering solutions to the borrower.

By starting this process, you've created a very definite and extremely serious deadline. As this deadline approaches, the pressure on the borrower will mount.

If you can stay cool and continue to focus on the goal of developing a solution, you will usually be able to come to an agreement.

The longer a foreclosure will take, the easier it will be to find this solution. Foreclosure is something which hangs over a borrower's head like the blade of a guillotine. It's there, it's real and it will come crashing down very soon.

In states like New York, you might have two or three years to work with the borrower while the foreclosure is being processed. To put it simply, you don't need to worry about what will happen when the process is finished because you have so much time to work on avoiding it.

You should never be afraid to initiate this process. If you've hired an attorney you can trust and you've filled every requirement up to this point, then there is nothing to prevent you from starting the process.

In my experience, most borrowers will finally agree to a solution before they are evicted so you shouldn't be afraid of it going all the way through either. Foreclosure is just a tool and one which has been very useful.

Dealing with the Senior Lien

Even though taking possession of your borrower's home is a rare occurrence it is a possibility and I want to cover an important topic. When you become the owner of the home after foreclosing from a second lien position, there will be a "Subject-to" clause in the first loan paperwork.

What this means is you now own the property "subject-to" the first mortgage. You own this house but there is still a first mortgage on it.

This can be a tricky situation. When this happens, the senior lender will likely contact you. They will normally not be happy about having the house taken out from under them and they will still want the money they're owed.

At this point, you are no longer dealing with a borrower but a lender. The tables have turned and you are now in the same position the borrower was just a few months before.

I've actually dealt with this situation a number of times. I've received phone calls from the owner of the senior lien and they've been rather mad about what just happened. They want their money and they are going to try to get it from me.

What I've found to be the best option at this point is to take the place of the borrower and try to work with the original lender.

I've purchased a lot of non performing notes. I've handled nearly every problem you might run into. My credit is excellent and I have multiple sources of steady and reliable income.

To put it another way, I should be the perfect borrower in the eyes of a bank. Giving me a loan is virtually risk free and I have far more assets than the original borrower.

When I get this phone call I will then try to explain the situation. I will tell them how I purchased the note, tried to work with the borrower and was left with no other option. Most banks will understand this because they're in the same exact business. I will then try to explain my intentions from this point forward.

Now that I own the home, I will need to make my money back in some way. The best way to do this is to hold onto the house and turn it into a rental property. While I may have been trying to get monthly payments from the borrower, I can generally get the same payment from a renter.

This makes it so I am now a landlord, complete with all the hassles and obligations, but I will still make my money back.

Since I am just renting it out, I will still own the house after my original investment has been paid off. I can then sell it for potential profit.

In order to do this, however, I will need to make payments on or get rid of the senior lien. What I do is offer to work with them. I prove that I have wonderful credit, am experienced in real estate management and want to work with the lender.

I offer to make the same payments they expected from the borrowers but I promise to do so on time, every month, until the loan is paid off.

The reason they accept this is from time to time is that many lenders weren't receiving any payments from the borrower at all. This person may have been delinquent for a number of months, even years, and the lender was receiving nothing.

By accepting this agreement to work with me, the lender has now swapped an unreliable borrower for someone who not only can but will make diligent payments on the loan.

This can be a great way to handle the holder of the senior lien. In most cases this will be a bank but you may find the senior lien is also owned by an investor.

No matter who owns it, they might be open to begin receiving money from the loan and you might be their best option. Doing this might switch the entire dynamic of the original investment but it will still allow us to make a profit.

The First Mortgage Can Foreclose

I've covered what to do when you foreclose from junior position and then get contacted by the holder of the senior lien but it's important to remember the first can foreclose as well.

The first mortgage is called the senior lien because it's first in line. If the property were to be liquidated and all the loans paid off, the first mortgage would get the first portion of the equity payment and all liens junior to this loan will have to split the remainder.

Banks are foreclosing less and less these days. These banks have a reputation to uphold and foreclosure is a matter of public record. If they began foreclosing on every property which is a few months behind on payments, their reputation would plummet.

Investors would be able to see how often this lender's loans fall apart and might stop doing business with them.

Banks will, however, still foreclose from time to time. This is especially true for any loan which is a few years late on payments. The bank has determined that this person will likely never start paying back their mortgage so they have no other option. When they do this, they're generally not obligated to inform the owners of the junior liens.

This is why staying up to date on the status of the

senior lien is so important. The bank could begin foreclosure proceedings and you might never know. They don't have to tell you so the only way you'll stay informed is by staying on top of things.

You can do this by checking PACER records, running credit checks on the borrower, and including a provision in the work-out agreement which states that the borrower must keep you informed.

The fact that the first can foreclose is also part of the reason why your work-out solution needs to fit into your borrower's budget. If your monthly payments on the junior lien are too high, the borrower may be forced to skip a few payments on their first mortgage.

This can essentially force the bank to initiate foreclosure and attempt to take the house.

Information is important for every step of investing in non performing notes. You will be sorting through a lot of information when you're choosing the notes. You will need more information for the Wake-up and Work-out.

Once things have been settled, however, your job is not finished. You need to stay on top of things until the loan is completely paid off.

This can be made easier by having a loan servicing company handle your notes and this will be covered in the coming chapters.

Friend and Foe

Foreclosure has become a dirty word in the lending markets of today. While it was once simply a way to collect on a delinquent debt, it is now seen as predatory and many consider it as a form of thievery.

This perception is fairly inaccurate but it is a good example of how the public feels about this process. Many first time note investors want to avoid foreclosure as much as they can.

We don't really want to own the property, this much is true, but we do need to find a way to get our borrower to start paying us the money they owe. In most cases, a solution can be created before foreclosure becomes a necessity.

In other cases, however, we simply have no other option but to begin and threaten it. Foreclosure is both the last and best option we have.

You will rarely, if ever, actually complete a foreclosure. We could, in fact, consider this as a worst case scenario in the junior lien niche. Foreclosure may be the last solution we want but it is still a solution.

When you foreclose you are still able to make a profit. Your money is not gone. The only thing that has changed is the way in which you will make your money.

The entire process of foreclosure can cost money. There are legal fees, publishing costs, and money lost while the borrower continues to avoid you.

Since most foreclosures will end in a work-out and all of the missed payments have been accumulating in arrears, however, there is virtually nothing to lose by initiating foreclosure. Even if you have to go through with it, you will still be in a great position to make a profit.

To make things even better, you've managed to purchase this property for pennies on the dollar because your note cost so much less than the fair market value of the house.

You'll find that you can purchase a note for $2,000, for example, but it's tied to a house worth $150,000. You've only had to pay a few thousand dollars (an option fee) for the right to foreclose on a valuable property.

I mention all of this to further illustrate how the threat of foreclosure can be very useful. It may be our last choice but it's not a bad choice. And more importantly, we were forced into it.

Before you even begin thinking about foreclosure you will have already tried a number of different ways to create a solution for your borrower.

They were the one who refused to work with you. They have turned down every offer of help and now they've left you with no other option.

Generally speaking, it's the borrower who has decided on foreclosure and not you.

Just as foreclosure can be a great tool for us, it is also useful for the owner of the senior lien. They will generally have even more invested in this borrower than you do and might be very motivated to make a portion of their money back. The senior lien holder is legally allowed to foreclose once the provisions have been met.

This means foreclosure can be both a friend and a foe. While it may be a great solution for us, when all other options have failed, it can be a problem if the senior lien holder decides to foreclose. To avoid any problems associated with this possibility, you simply need to stay informed. Foreclosure by the senior lien can be seem like something to fear but it is not as big a problem as you think.

In some areas, it can take years for a foreclosure to go through. During this time, you will continue to try to work with the borrower.

Now that they know they're being foreclosed on by the senior lien, they are often more willing to find an actual solution to their problems. There have been multiple instances where I managed to work out a solution with the borrower before the senior lien's foreclosure went through.

Foreclosure can be both good and bad but, no matter what, it's not really something to be afraid of. Junior liens that you will need to foreclose on are rare.

Notes which actually go all the way through the process are rarer still. In my experience, successful work-outs far outnumber notes which require foreclosure.

Moving Forward

So far, this book has covered some of the basics of note investing as well as some of a note investor's greatest fears. Now that you understand how little you have to fear and how profitable this investment can be, you might be excited to begin purchasing non performing notes.

Before you do, however, I want to cover something which is an important element in any successful note investment.

I handle a lot of notes. There is no way I can personally take care of everything relating to each note in my portfolio. Since each note needs some periodic attention, however, I will usually send them out to a loan servicer.

This person is an expert in dealing with these sorts of situations and can be one of the most valuable assets you have.

The next chapter will explain what loan servicing is and how it can help you.

CHAPTER TEN:

Loan Servicing for Non-Performing and Re-Performing Junior Liens

The previous chapters have given you a detailed look into the world of notes. You've learned where they come from, how they're purchased, and what needs to be done to make a profit. I've also explained how some of your biggest fears might actually be some of your greatest assets.

Now, I would like to cover a topic which many people find hard to understand.

When you purchase a note, your work is just beginning. You will need to get the borrower to work with you and then come up with a solution.

Once a solution has been reached, you will need to stay on top of the loan and make sure everything is handled correctly for the life of the note. This is where loan servicing comes into play.

What is Loan Servicing?

When you invest in real estate, there is a lot to worry about. Every property will need regular maintenance and you are responsible for all repairs.

Making these repairs on time is vital because failure to do so will give your tenants an excuse to stop paying rent. Anyone who has ever owned a home can tell you how prone they are to a variety of problems.

If you were an active real estate investor then you would likely own multiple properties. Dealing with the regular maintenance and repairs required by these properties can exceed your ability to handle them personally.

What most real estate investors do is hire a property management company. This company will then take care of all the repairs and maintenance, billing and collections, etc. that a rental property might need.

A loan servicing company is like a property management company. When you own a lot of notes, you'll have a lot to worry about.

If you want to keep all of your notes performing then you will need to stay in contact with the borrowers. Your relationship is not over once the work-out solution has been agreed to.

Every month you will need to collect payments from all of your borrowers. You should also send them a letter or email each month that updates them on the current status of the loan.

You'll want to let them know how much is paid off and what portion of their last payment went to the interest and which went to pay down the principle. When tax season comes, you will need to file a 1098 which requires some effective bookkeeping.

All of this can amount to a lot of work. If you only handle a few notes, it might not be a big deal. As you progress and eventually own a larger pile of these notes, however, the monthly work begins to build up.

While you can handle this yourself, if you wanted to, many investors choose to hire a loan servicing company.

This company will then handle all of the monthly work for you while you focus on finding and fixing new profitable investments.

The Middle-Man

When you hire a loan servicing company, they will essentially become the middle-man. Their position is between you and the borrower and they will handle all correspondence and contacts between the two of you.

When you have a lot of notes at any one time, this servicer also becomes a central location from which to monitor the current status off all your notes.

Many loan servicing companies will have their own software which you can use to follow your investments. These may be web-based or will have some other convenient method of access.

This can be a great asset for anyone with a large portfolio of notes. Rather than needing to keep files on each borrower, you can simply contact your servicer to make sure everything is going well.

Most loan servicing companies will charge a set monthly fee for each note. This is generally rather low and should not really impact your profits significantly. The time and money they save you will easily pay for the service itself.

It is, however, important to keep in mind that some servicing companies will be handling notes for a large number of investors and this can affect how personal your relationship with them is.

They will collect the monthly payments on every note

and then send it to you. This makes things a bit easier for everyone involved because each one of your borrowers will be sending their payments to the same place.

The loan servicer should also be keeping detailed notes of these transactions. When tax season rolls around, you can simply call up and request the financial information you need.

A loan servicer can also be instructed to keep the borrower up to date. They will send out a statement each month which gives the borrower a full report on the status of their loan.

This will include how much is still owed, how much is owed in interest, how much longer the loan will be active, and other important information.

This helps your borrower avoid any surprises. They will always be aware of when their next payment is due and how much they will need to pay before the loan is finished.

Your borrower will have every last bit of information regarding their loan and can request more at any time. They can receive a statement from the servicer just as they would from a bank and this helps make you seem more professional.

Overall, a loan servicing company is not a requirement. You can handle all of your notes alone and many people choose to do this. Hiring a servicing company, however, will simply make your life easier.

The more notes you have, the more there is to worry about. Handing your notes over to a loan servicer is simply a way to outsource this routine maintenance. It's not something you have to do but it can be a good idea when you've found it hard to juggle so many notes at once.

Servicing vs. Collections

There is a misconception I often run into with people new to the world of notes and I want to clear it up right now. I talk about investing in notes quite a lot.

Most people are intrigued by the prospect and the money which can be made. One mistake they often make, however, is thinking that they can just outsource everything.

They think they can purchase a non-performing note and then hand it over to someone else. This person, they think, will handle the wake-up and work-out process for them. They can purchase notes and then sit back, relax and wait for the money to start rolling in.

This, as you will now learn, is not what a loan servicer does.

Investing in non-performing junior liens is a very high-touch, relationship-oriented business. I make my money from the relationship I build with my borrowers and not from some obscure legal obligation. Investing in these notes is also a bit of a niche market.

There are not as many people handling junior liens as senior liens and first mortgages. This is especially true for most loan servicing companies.

These companies will generally handle non-performing senior liens—which are first mortgages, more often than not. These are expensive and represent quite a lot of money.

Senior liens differ from junior liens in that they focus on the collateral more than the borrower.

Some loan servicing companies will handle collections for non-performing senior liens. The problem for us, however, is that this is a completely different process. The leverage used for a senior lien is the collateral which means they will be threatening foreclosure to get the borrower to start paying.

This is fairly impersonal and doesn't necessarily require much of a relationship with the borrower.

To put it simply, most of these loan servicing companies just don't understand our methods. They aren't used to building up a personal relationship with the borrower and they will generally not care if the person starts paying back the loan or gets evicted.

A loan servicing agent gets paid every month no matter what happens to the loan.

This is why I say you have to handle the wake-up and work-out yourself. While you may find a loan servicing company which can file a Notice of Default or help you initiate foreclosure, they won't help you build a personal relationship with your borrower.

More importantly, they are indifferent to whether or not a beneficial solution is created.

This relationship becomes even more important later on. Anything can happen and a borrower may begin to miss payments again. If you have a personal relationship with them then you can call them up, find out what happened, and come up with a new solution.

A loan servicing company will not do this. They will send out a bill, send a demand letter and continue to request payment but that is all they'll do.

To Outsource or Not

Now that I've covered the difference between collections and servicing, I want to focus on whether or not you should outsource your loan servicing. The main theme with junior liens is personal interaction.

These investments work because of your personal relationship with the people who will be paying you money.

You already know how important it is to personally handle the wake-up and work-out but it can be hard to tell when to keep doing everything yourself.

Generally speaking, it is better to handle everything on your own. The old saying, "If you want something done right, do it yourself" is especially true when it comes to junior liens.

When you handle the wake-up yourself then you know everything about how to contact the borrower. Handling the work-out yourself means you have all of the borrower's financial information and a keen insight into their current life.

If you don't outsource the continued servicing of the loan you will always be well-informed and have control over what is said and done.

Outsourcing this servicing, however, will take you out of the loop. The servicer will be the only one with direct and regular contact with the borrower.

You will have spent all of this time and effort establishing a relationship, building trust and developing an understanding only to take yourself out of the picture once the borrower has agreed to start paying.

There's no way to tell what can go wrong in any given situation and this is no different. A borrower may have gotten sick or injured or lost their job. They might stop paying for no reason and you have to rely on the servicer to let you know.

Servicing companies are very busy. They may be handling hundreds or thousands of notes and can seldom afford to make any one of them a priority.

When something goes wrong, you need to know right away. You can't let the borrower start to lag behind in payments. You have to let them know that you are always on top of things. The only way to make sure you always know what is going on with each note is to service it yourself.

Some of the notes you purchase may be simple. The wake-up and work-out will go quickly and the borrower is perfectly happy to keep paying. This type of person pays on time every month and you never have to worry about them.

This type of note only needs a little babysitting and it can be the perfect candidate for a loan servicer. So really, if there is any doubt at all, you should consider handling it yourself.

Note Smith Servicing Software

Servicing your own notes is a lot easier than it sounds. If everything goes according to plan, each note should only require a few minutes of work each month.

All you really need to do is collect the payment and send out a statement. Even though this is hardly more than a few hours' worth of work each month for someone with quite a few notes, I have found a few tools which make it even easier.

Let's say you've purchased a number of different notes, contacted the borrowers, and came to an agreement. All of your notes are performing now and all you need to worry about is continued servicing.

Your biggest concern at this point is keeping track of everything. You want to make sure all of the relevant information is easy to access and review.

While you can do this with an overly-complicated spreadsheet, Note Smith is a note servicing program which has been designed specifically for this type of investment. It was created by someone who is a note investor himself and was made to help people service their own notes. It is an incredibly easy-to-use program and it can help make your life much easier.

Who to Hire

Hopefully you will become so successful at investing in notes that you'll find yourself with hundreds of them in your portfolio. At this point, servicing them yourself is no longer an option.

I handle many notes and I've been forced to hire my own personal in-house servicers. This may not be an option for you and so it's important to know how to find a reputable servicing company when the time comes.

Here are a few criteria which should help you find the best servicing company:

References

I've always relied on word of mouth and I think this is a good place to start. As you become more involved in the world of notes you'll begin to meet other investors. These people can be a great resource when it comes to finding a servicing company.

Ask around and try to get some recommendations. If multiple people suggest the same company then you might have found a good one.

Experience

When contacting different servicing companies, it can be a good idea to ask about their experience. Some companies will specialize in one type of loan or another. You will, of course, want to find one which deals with mortgages. If they have experience dealing with re-performing junior liens, (which is rare) this is even better.

Remember that junior lien investing is a bit of a niche market and it can be hard to find a servicing company which actually understands your unique needs.

Cost

As with most things in life, there will be a cost associated with hiring a loan servicing company. Most of these companies will offer reasonable rates and this is generally about $10 - $20 per note each month. This is a very small fraction of our monthly payments and can be negligible.

Other companies, however, may charge $100 a month for each note and this can seriously impact our profits. Make sure to factor the servicing cost into your profit predictions.

If I can give you one piece of advice it would be to do plenty of research before choosing a servicing company. Not every servicer is as good as the last one and dealing with a bad servicer can be disastrous.

To get the most out of your note investments you'll have to trust your servicer but, before you do, you have to make sure they are worthy of this trust. Never settle for the first servicing company you find.

Moving Forward

At this point you have a detailed understanding of basic non performing note investing. You've also gained some keen insight into how non performing note investing might work.

One problem many people run into, however, is what to do with the notes in their portfolio to maximize your long term earnings potential.

The solution to this is simple. It is also, incidentally, a good way to find money to begin investing in notes. Many people have an Individual Retirement Account (IRA) and few ever really know what to do with it.

The next chapter will focus on how IRAs can be a great companion to notes and what type of IRA might be the best option.

CHAPTER ELEVEN:

Taxes and the Re-Performing Junior Lien

At this point, you understand how and why investing in notes can be a great way to start building your own personal wealth. I've covered everything from what to look for to how to fix and service a note.

What I want to focus on now is an important topic for anyone entering into the world of note investing.

If you move forward, you will eventually find yourself in possession of re-performing junior liens. You've worked everything out and your borrower is happily making payments every month.

Eventually, you will likely have a nice collection of re-performing notes and you will need to know what to do with them.

Taxes and Notes

The only real reason you'll be investing in notes is to make yourself money. Ideally, you'll reinvest a portion of this money to continue increasing your profits. At a certain point, you may be making quite a bit of money every month.

Let's say, for example, you have purchased and worked on a number of different notes.

You now find yourself with 10 re-performing notes which are each bringing in about $300 a month per note. If we do the math, this amounts to an extra $36,000 a year on top of your other sources of income. This is a conservative estimate but it works well as an example.

If you already have a significant income stream coming from a job or your own business, adding $36,000 a year can bump you up into a higher tax bracket.

This might change everything about the way you handle your taxes and finances.

Things will begin to change if this happens, and keeping track of everything can get complicated. In addition to this, moving into a higher tax bracket can lead you to paying more in taxes as well as being restricted from certain tax breaks or government programs.

This might seem inevitable and having too much money is never a bad problem but there is still a way to avoid this.

Presenting the IRA

People will often ask me what my goal is with investing in notes. They are sometimes a little confused when I give them my answer, so I will explain it detail over the next few pages.

I always tell them my goal is to grow my own personal self-directed IRA and I do this by placing my re-performing notes into it.

An IRA is an Individual Retirement Account and many people all over the country will have one. It is essentially

148

a way to begin saving for retirement by utilizing investments to generate a profit.

People will generally place a certain portion of their yearly income into an IRA. This money is then used to purchase investments which will increase the overall value of the account.

Most traditional IRAs are handled and managed by a custodian. This person is placed in charge of using the money in the account to make investments.

The profits from these investments will go back into the account and are used to increase the account's value. Most of the time, these investments are things like stocks and mutual funds—very common types of investments.

Generally speaking, you will need to reach a certain age before you can begin withdrawing money from the IRA without incurring penalties. The age is 70½ years old. By this time, most people will have retired and can rely on the money in their IRA to do so in comfort.

And that is just for the required withdrawals. Other taxable withdrawals can be made as desired as early as 59 ½.

Taxes and the IRA

While saving for retirement is important and an IRA can be a great way to do it, there are other benefits for us as investors. The money for the IRA investments will usually come out of your paycheck.

The difference, however, is that the proceeds will come before taxes are taken out. These are "before tax" deductions which means the money placed into the account is not taxed.

In other words, let's say you made $40,000 per year. If

you put $10,000 into your IRA, then you would only be taxed for $30,000. There may be some taxes to pay when you eventually withdraw money from the account, but until then, the money is essentially tax-free.

This allows you to utilize more of your compounding yearly earnings to save for retirement.

The biggest benefit, however, is that the profits from the IRA investments are not taxed either. All of the money you place into the account is protected by the IRA umbrella. When your IRA makes a profit from its investments, this extra money will go back into the account and is used to purchase more investments.

The money you make by doing this is not counted towards your yearly income as far as the IRS is concerned.

No matter how much money you make from the IRA, you won't have to worry about changing tax brackets. If you took those 10 re-performing notes from the example above and put them into an IRA, that $36,000 per year would not be taxed and could be used to purchase more investments.

While you may not be able to spend the profit you make from these notes, you will be able to hold onto more of it and still use it to follow this note strategy of reinvesting.

The Downside

Most traditional IRAs will consist of investments in things like stocks and mutual funds. Note investing is not something they embrace. These more traditional investment options are seen as being safer and more reliable despite the smaller profit margin.

Taking Control

Most people choose to use a basic IRA because it is so

simple. All they need to do is put a certain amount of money into the account each month. The rest of the work is handled by the custodian/manager.

While this can make saving for retirement incredibly easy, we've seen why traditional IRAs are not as effective as we would like.

Fortunately, there is another option which lets us enjoy all of the benefits of a traditional IRA while still being able to invest in notes and quickly grow our personal wealth. The best option for anyone investing in notes is a *self-directed* IRA.

The key difference between a traditional IRA and a self-directed one is who will be in charge of the account.

Rather than utilizing a custodian to make all of the decisions for us, a self-directed IRA allows you to take control. You can use the money in your account to purchase nearly any type of investment you can think of.

Instead of simply spending your own money to purchase notes and then declaring the profits as income, you can use the money in your own self directed IRA to purchase notes and send the profit back into the account.

You'll be able to avoid the taxes you would normally need to pay while gaining significantly more money to invest in new notes. These new notes can stay in your IRA and exponentially increase your retirement savings.

Switching to a self-directed IRA will, of course, require a bit more work. Fortunately, this is not any more work than you'd be doing if you were investing in notes without an IRA.

You will essentially be doing the same thing, following the same strategies I've outlined in this book, but you will be avoiding tax problems at the same time.

The only drawback to using a self-directed IRA is that you can't simply remove the money and spend it without incurring a penalty. When you take money out of the account too early, there will be some penalties.

In addition to that, you will then need to pay taxes on the money because it has become income.

Roth IRAs

Money placed into a Roth IRA is taxed before it goes into the account. This money is essentially handled in the same way as any of your income and the IRS will take a portion of it.

Once this money has been taxed, however, you will not have to pay taxes on it when you eventually withdraw it from the IRA.

More importantly, the profits made by the IRA's investments will still not be taxed and will continue to be covered by the protections of the IRA.

This can be great when you're dealing with a long-term strategy. Since we're talking about saving for retirement, you might be looking at a few decades worth of investing before you're done.

Making money in the short term is always great but it's important to keep one eye on the future as well. There will come a day when you will withdraw the money from your IRA and retire. When you do, a Roth IRA will make the process much easier.

More importantly, you will greatly reduce the amount of taxes you'll have to pay.

Since you've already paid your taxes before putting the money in the account, you'll be paying far less when you eventually withdraw the money.

You won't have to worry about different tax brackets and you'll end up with a larger retirement nest egg at the end of the rainbow.

When to Think About an IRA

I always tell people they should keep things as simple as possible in the beginning. There is a lot to consider when you first enter the world of notes and it can be hard to wrap your mind around everything if the process is too complicated.

Most people will start by purchasing a small number of notes and working them out. This will make them a small profit and they will likely do it again.

Once you've decided note investing is your preferred method of wealth creation, however, it's time to start thinking about IRAs. The way these accounts work means you'll receive the greatest benefit by starting them as early as possible.

The sooner you start adding notes into your IRA, the sooner you can begin utilizing the benefits of the account.

The choice between a regular or Roth IRA is really up to you, but it's important to consider the benefits of each option before choosing one. An IRA which is made up of successful note investments is the easiest and safest way to begin planning for retirement.

You will be able to follow every strategy in this book within your IRA. Nothing really changes except the way the money is handled.

Rather than going into your checking account, the profits will be used to continue growing your portfolio.

What this means for you is your IRA will grow exponentially tax free or tax deferred. Each successful investment will then create more potential investments to grow the same way.

Moving Forward

Now you have the information needed to begin creating your own wealth through investing in non performing notes.

I've covered common problems and offered some advice as well as a variety of different strategies and approaches to this business.

With all of this information at your disposal, you can now begin investing and growing your own portfolio.

Be a "ONE PERCENTER" – take these ideas and actually go out and make it happen.

To your success,

The "Voice of Reason",

Gordon Moss

Quixote Ventures, Inc.

Visit RealEstateAndNoteInvesting.com for a special message from Gordon

Made in the USA
San Bernardino, CA
28 March 2016